The Story of Enstone

Devised and Edited by Graham Binns

The Story of Enstone

Devised and Edited by **Graham Binns**

THE ENSTONE LOCAL HISTORY CIRCLE

First published in 1999 by The Enstone Local History Circle

© The Enstone Local History Circle 1999

ISBN 0 9537423 0 X

All rights reserved. No part of this publication may be reproduced, stored in a retrieval system, or transmitted in any form or by any means, electronic, mechanical photocopying, or otherwise without the prior written permission of the Enstone Local History Circle.

A CIP record for this title is available from the British Library.

Acknowledgements: To Sheila Stewart for permission to quote from *Lifting the Latch*. To C. J. Bond and Messrs Blackwell for permission to reproduce the plan of the site of the medieval village at Lower Chalford. To the National Monuments Record/English Heritage for the use of the photograph of Enstone in 1930. To Tom Miller, Enstone Flying School, for the courtesy of the flight from which the photograph of Enstone in 1999 was taken. Field Names Map prepared for publication by Richard Garratt.

Typeset by Neil Curtis Publishing Services.

Designed by **Mark-making design**, Chipping Norton.

Printed and bound in Britain by Biddles Limited, Guildford and King's Lynn.

Contents

Preface	8
The Parish	10
Ditchley and Heythrop	10
Change, Decay, and Conversion	12
Developments	13
Housing	13
Enstone Airfield	14
Amenities	15
Neat Enstone	16
The Fantastical Mr Bushell, Queen Henrietta's Waterworks, and Robert Southey's Cheeses	19
The Character of Thomas Bushell	22
Adams' Stores and Naboth's Vineyard	22
Mr Jolly and His Ricks – A Moral Tale	24
Church Enstone	26
St Kenelm and His Church	31
The Rectory Barn	34
Chalford	36
Cleveley	38
Fulwell	42
Gagingwell	44
Lidstone	46

Radford 47
Deserted and Shrunken Medieval Villages 48
Water-mills 55
The Naming of Places 57
The Naming of Persons 60
Ladies Bountiful 62
Tales from Horace 64
    Patience Taplin and the Mice 64
    How to Catch a Hare 65
    Catching the Post 65
The *Enstone Ensign* 67
The Early History of Enstone 69
    Palaeolithic, Mesolithic, and Neolithic Periods 70
    Bronze Age 72
    The Iron Age 73
    The Roman Period 74
Farming in the Parish 76
Field Names 78
The Natural History of Enstone 80
    Introduction 80
    Climate and Habitats 81
    Birds of Enstone 82
    Wild Flowers of Enstone 85
    Other Wildlife 87
Other Reading 92
Published Sources 93
Enstone in 1854 94

Illustrations

Cover:
    The Hoarstone..Susan Garrington
Line drawings by Andrea Bates:
    The Allotments, Spring Hill, before the low-cost housing 13
    The Litchfield Arms 16
    The Wells, Enstone 20
    Adams' Stores 23
    The Drive with Cow Parsley, Church Enstone 26
    Five Chimneys, Church Enstone 27
    The Thatch, Church Enstone 29
    The Mill House, Church Enstone 30
    The bridlepath that was a turnpike, Cleveley 40
    Fulwell 42
    Lidstone 46
    Radford 47
    Cleveley, the line of the fence follows the line of the leat to the mill 55
  Settlement Earthworks – Nether Chalford, by C. J. Bond 51
  Birds – from engravings by Thomas Bewick
  and from Wood's *Natural History*..82-4
Inside back cover
    Field Names Map – Enstone Local History Circle
Back cover
    A Cake and Ale Feast
Centre Fold
    Photographs of The Church Porch, The Rectory barn, Machinery at Enstone Mill, and Enstone from the air in 1999, by Terence Wright.
    Photograph of Enstone in 1930 from the National Monuments Record.

Preface

The aim has been to produce an account that is informative and entertaining. I apologize in advance for errors and omissions of substance.

I have drawn heavily on the recollections of Mont Abbott as written by Sheila Stewart. Another valuable source of information and anecdote has been a typescript memorandum sent to R. T. Lattey, then Chairman of the Enstone Local History Circle, by Horace Adams in 1961. Adams was born in Enstone in 1885, the younger son of James Joseph Adams. The latter had worked in his father's village store in Bladon, and then set up on his own at Enstone. Horace Adams provided background to the story of the famous feud between his father and the 16th Viscount Dillon. Horace himself had a successful career, becoming a Freeman of the City of London. During World War II he set up and organized the Army Mechanics Training School. The History Circle's archive has provided useful material – particularly from two albums put together years ago by Miss Winifred Bennett. These, by the way, were photographed page by page for the County Archives and can be consulted there.

Andrea Bates, whose pictorial record of the parish is an archive in itself, has contributed the pen and ink drawings that ornament the text.

Roger Field, President of the History Circle, has provided much information and advice, and I am glad to acknowledge help from Davina Huxley (particularly relating to Church Enstone), Margaret Wearing, whose family has been long established here, Dennis Foster, who is leaving the neighbourhood, Jennifer Candy, who is a new arrival, and Jillian Binns. Our cover, The Hoarstone, is by Susan Garrington.

Charles Powell has organized the financing of the project and has contributed some helpful notes on the church. Robin Newson has written the sections covering the early history of the parish, the deserted villages, and a note on water-mills. Neil Curtis has contributed the overview of the natural history. Robert Parsons, whose family has for a long time farmed in the parish, has provided the section on farming. Local history is largely unwritten and must rely upon the recollections of those who have lived a generation or more in the parish. I would especially mention the Circle's indebtedness to Mrs Kitty Huckin, Mr Ernie Bartlett, Mr Nigel Eley, Mr Joe Arthur, Mr Ken Kench, Mr Len Reynolds, and the late Mr Charlie Sheffield.

C. J. Bond, an archaeologist who has made several studies locally, gave helpful advice and has permitted us to reproduce here his drawing of the site of the deserted village at Lower Chalford.

All this has been put on to disk and seen through to the design stage by Neil Curtis, who also made the arrangements for publication. *The Story of Enstone* is intended as The Enstone Local History Circle's particular celebration of the year AD 2000, and any profits from the sale of copies will be devoted to the parish.

I have referred to the financing of the book. This has been effected through loans generously made by individuals, and their practical help in this way is gratefully acknowledged.

Graham Binns

The Parish

Enstone, in West Oxfordshire, occupies the second largest Parish Council area in the county, 5019 hectares (just over 19 square miles). It includes the villages of Neat and Church Enstone, and the settlements of Broadstonehill, Chalford, Cleveley, Fulwell, Gagingwell, Lidstone, and Radford. It is about 9 kilometres (5½ miles) in length and, at its widest, about 4 km (2½ miles) Its centre lies 28 km (17½ miles) north-west of the city of Oxford. Neat Enstone is in the middle of that part of the parish which is bisected by the main road (A44) from Oxford to Stratford. It contains the Primary School, the Village Sports and Social Club, the Youth Hall, the Parish Hall, the Post Office Shop, and The Harrow Inn. Church Enstone, on the hill above, lies near the Bicester road. St Kenelm's, the parish church, has an original foundation in the ninth century.

The 1991 census recorded 1078 persons occupying 437 households within the parish boundary.

Ditchley and Heythrop

Domesday records Winchcomb Abbey as holding 24 hides (2880 acres/1166 hectares) of arable land in Enstone. The Abbey remained the dominant landowner, increasing its holdings, until the dissolution of the monasteries. After that the first Lord of the Manor was Sir Thomas Pope, founder of Trinity College, Oxford. Then followed three successive Earls of Downe until 1668. A sister of the last of these had married Sir Francis Henry Lee of Ditchley and, on that Earl's death, the manor passed to the Ditchley family. The Lees, by marriage, became Lee-Dillons (or Dillon-Lees). The Lees became Earls of Litchfield and the Dillons viscounts – which is why both names crop up from time to time in relation to Enstone. The 17th Viscount died in 1932 and Ditchley, which owned much land in the parish of Enstone as well as in Spelsbury (where the house stands) passed to Mr Ronald

Tree. Winston Churchill frequently stayed at Ditchley Park in the 1940s, and the principles of the Land-Lease Agreement were worked out in the house. In the spirit of this Anglo-American co-operation, Sir David Wills, the last owner, gave the house to the Ditchley Foundation, set up to study matters of common interest to the peoples of Britain and the United States.

The other great house which had land in the parish, though, like Ditchley, it lies outside the bounds, is Heythrop. Formerly the property of the Earls of Shrewsbury, this was purchased in the nineteenth century by the Brasseys, then became a Roman Catholic seminary, and now, in its latest guise, a staff college for the National Westminster Bank.

The Ditchley Foundation, the Ditchley Estate, and the National Westminster Bank Staff Training College all provide employment locally in Enstone.

Change, Decay, and Conversion

In 1843 the residents of Church Enstone (listed here as heads of families) were: the vicar, the churchwarden, three farmers, a carpenter who was also parish clerk; a tailor, a miller, a baker, a blacksmith, three shoemakers (?for horses), a collarmaker (?for horse collars), two shopkeepers, and many agricultural labourers.

At the beginning of the twentieth century, nine-tenths of the local population was still employed on the land or in work relating to agriculture. This went on up to and beyond World War I, but increasing mechanization drove the workforce into other industries, and a number of Enstonians took off as commuters to Cowley and to the new factories. 'It were' says Mont Abbott 'the days when men was already forsaking the allotments to garner higher wage in the motor industry.'

From about 1960 on, there began an infiltration of outsiders into the old community. They were sufficiently attracted to cottages without water-closets (which had been abandoned by their inhabitants for the conveniences of the council house) to spend large sums on conversion. The proximity of Charlbury railway station made the area attractive to those who could not quite abandon the diversions of London or Oxford. The improvement of the housing stock did not, fortunately, go so far as in a Gloucestershire village of which Duff Hart-Davies wrote 'I found it hard to imagine what the inhabitants *did*, so immaculate was the setting, with not a stone or lump of earth or blade of grass out of place among the parked Jaguars and BMWs'. Enstone is not a 'toy village' inhabited only by Posy Simmonds people, but it is still not that easy to find a farmer or an inhabitant who has anything to do with the land.

House prices were forced up beyond the reach of indigenous folk – especially the young – and it is only recently that anything has been done about that with low-cost housing. Any mild resentment that Old Enstonians may harbour might have been assuaged by time (old newcomers are now in turn looking sideways at newer-comers) and by such legislation as allowed the purchase of council houses. As the 1968 *Review* observed: 'not more than thirty per cent of the population are real Enstonians, but the old Chinese boast applies – if you stay long enough you become Chinese!'

Developments
Housing

The Enstone Village Appraisal (1995) noted that the first council housing to be built was in The Drive during the 1920s with more being

The Allotments, Spring Hill

built in Cleveley Road, Quarry Close, and Chapel Lane in the decade after World War II.[1]

Then came Litchfield Close and The Spinneys, now extended into Braybrooke Close. All these amount to more than fifty private houses in Neat Enstone in addition to the council housing. Low-cost houses have been built at Clay Hill Close behind The Drive where ECHO (Enstone Community Housing Organization) has built eight 'starter' houses on a portion of the Spring Hill allotments on Bicester Road. Clay Hill is the area by the triangle between the Bicester Road and the A44. The houses, called Clay Hill Close, stand, in fact, upon Spring Hill. There are further proposals to build ECHO houses on the corner of Cox's Lane and the Lidstone Road, but the siting of these has led to opposition.

Enstone Airfield

Marked 'disused' on the map, the airfield was, up to the late 1970s, early 1980s partly farmed. The runways were used by a gliding club, the Enstone Eagles. There followed, however, the development of the site into an industrial estate, much of it in low profile with the striking exception of a 96-feet (29-metre) high animal feed mill. These developments were followed in 1982 by the advent of microlight aircraft, or motorized gliders. While these added a kind of Heath-Robinson animation to otherwise vacant skyscapes, they also made a persistent whine throughout their leisurely flights over the parish.

Church Enstone and Gagingwell suffered most. The residents set up the Enstone District Environment Group to focus and co-ordinate protests to the planning authority, the West Oxfordshire District Council (WODC). A Department of the Environment enquiry in the Parish Hall on 1 April 1984 resulted in the Inspector upholding the WODC's refusal 'to grant an Established Use Certificate for the use of runway 2 for take-off and landing of light aircraft and gliders'. But the Inspector saw no objection in principle to the use of the airfield for flying purposes at the level that existed before 1980. This dictum gave room for further disputes over the ensuing years, but the microlights are heard less often. It is true that permission was given to allow a vintage Bristol freighter to use runway 1 in 1996 but it crashed on take-off, fortunately hurting no-one but itself. The latest use (some say abuse) of the runways is for Drive-it-All which permits enthusiasts to make the most of wheels.

1 James Ivings in 1960, when he was eighty-four: 'I didn't care for them [the council houses] at first. I'd lived in my old home for fifty years, when it was condemned. But I've changed my mind. Baths and hot-water and all the comforts of a modern home are nice to have in your old age.'

On another corner of the airfield, near the Great Tew road, a chicken factory has been built. The airfield industries provide employment. So do such developments as the conversion of Heythrop House into the Staff College for the National Westminster Bank.

Amenities

The Parish Hall was opened in 1922. Mont Abbott remarked: 'Our Hall may not seem much of a corrugated-iron effort nowadays compared to all they posh Community Centres that have cropped up in other villages since the Second World War, but to us in the let-down 'twenties it were a wonderful lift-up . . .' Smaller village groups still use the hall but there is now a much larger Youth Hall and a vibrant Sports and Social Club. But where once there were six, there are now only two pubs, The Crown in Church Enstone and The Harrow in Neat Enstone.

'Enstone County Primary School' became Enstone Primary School after 1 September 1999, the new designation allowing for greater participation of parents on the governing body. The old school house at Neat Enstone, which is still the hub of the school, was built in 1875. Until 1921, there had been a school for younger children at Church Enstone. After that date all the children went to Neat Enstone until further legislation required older children to go elsewhere.

Neat Enstone

~ ~ ◆ ~ ~

As you approach Neat Enstone from Woodstock, you come to Worth's garage on the site known generations ago as Jolly's Ricks. Worth's is a family service station, garage, and coach hire business, and its early years are so intimately related to Enstone that they should be recorded.

T. E. Worth started the business in 1923, mending bicycles, motor bicycles, and the few cars there were around. A year later he started a chauffeured service, taking five passengers at a time to the Wembley Exhibition in London for a fare of six shillings each, return. The next enterprise was the purchase of a sixteen-seater Morris Commercial which was turned into a school bus. Shortly after that he introduced a Saturday-Sunday run between Enstone and Oxford which brought girls who were in domestic service in the city home and back again. This was followed by a market-day service to Banbury.

Enstone was once called 'Enstone of the seven towns' – these being the settlements that surrounded it. There were also, in the coaching

The Litchfield Arms

days, seven inns. Only two remain, The Crown at Church Enstone and The Harrow at Neat Enstone. The Bell, which is on the left as you enter Neat Enstone after passing Worth's, was the last pub to close and, at one time, served the people from Cleveley after their Malt Shovel had gone. The Bell has now been converted to a private dwelling, but happily keeps its name.

The largest of the inns, and the one used by the coach trade in the early nineteenth century was The Litchfield Arms. The area it occupied above The Swan (now an unlicensed hotel) has been turned into houses and is called Litchfield Close. The coach trade declined with the coming of the railway to Charlbury, and the licence of The Litchfield Arms was then transferred to smaller premises, while the original inn was divided up. An occupant of part of it, one Jones, ran a bakery. On his death, James Joseph Adams, a Bladon man who had been running The Old Shop across the road, moved in and traded from there until his troubles with the 16th Viscount Dillon set in train the events that led to the setting up of Adams' Stores where that shop still stands today.[1]

The Talbot Inn, now Enstone House Residential Home, went through several transmutations as a dwelling house, being at different times a home for Colonel Dillon (a relation of the Viscount), a Mr Faulkner who owned the first motor in Enstone, and the famous John Jolly of the Ricks.[2] The Plough Inn adjoined the harness maker's at Hillside, opposite The Harrow.

Just by The Harrow is a straight tree-lined avenue, The Drive. This was laid down in 1889 by Albert Brassey as a handsome approach to the Lodge for Heythrop House. The Lodge itself had been built earlier, in 1877, from stone quarried at Heythrop. The Drive was barred and locked for twenty-four hours on 1 August each year. This continued until 1927, when new owners were in occupation and the house had been turned into St Bellarmimine's Jesuit College for the training of priests. They made over The Drive to the parish council, and council houses were built along the upper side of it in 1929.

Yew Tree House, above The Harrow on the slip road from Chipping Norton to Church Enstone (B4030), was a blacksmith's, last kept as such by a Mr Miles. The lane going down beside Adams' Stores had premises for a smith and for a wheelwright in the 1890s. The wheelwright, also a timber merchant, was named Baughan, and the blacksmith Hedges. The latter was notably skilful, being able to fashion a new iron tyre for a wagon wheel and forge-weld the two ends together in a complete circle, entirely unaided. The cottage on the hill, which

1 See the section: 'Adams' Stores and Naboth's Vineyard'.
2 See: 'Mr Jolly and His Ricks – A Moral Tale'.

still carries the sign 'The Old Shop', is now a dwelling. Originally five steps led up to the shop door but road widening swept them away and, in 1955 photographs, they have gone. In the 1880s The Old Shop was kept by a widow, Mrs Wells, who was helped by her daughter, Jennie. It was not so ambitious a store as Adams' became, but it sold some hardware, household requisites, a few cheap groceries, and sweets. After Jennie inherited the shop the story went about that two children who had rushed in to tell her that their mother had just borne twins were rewarded with a bull's-eye apiece, for Jennie abhorred extravagance. On her death the place became the Post Office for a time. Later, it was the home of R. T. Lattey, laboratory demonstrator turned historian, founder of the Enstone Local History Circle.

There used to be an elm on the green. It grew so massive and overreaching that it was thought a hazard and, in 1951, it was topped. After that operation it had the appearance of a gigantic shaving brush or a frayed rope's-end; its glory gone. It was doomed anyway and two decades later it succumbed, like 25 million other elms, to the scolytid beetle. A fine chestnut graces the green in its place.

In the mid-nineteenth century there were ninety-one houses in Neat Enstone and it had an adult population of 418. In 1997 the population had grown to 537 and the number of houses had significantly increased.

The Hoarstone which, as Enna's Stone, gives its name to Enstone is considered in its historical context in the section 'The Early History of Enstone'. It lies at the Charlbury and Fulwell road crossing near the Playing Field and 500 metres south-south-east of the church. When Edward Rudge wrote it up for *The Gentleman's Magazine* for February 1824, he gave its measurements: 'the large upright . . . is eight feet two inches, its greatest width is six feet ten inches, three feet six inches thick, ten feet nine inches from the top to its extremity under the soil.'

A century and more after Edward Rudge cleaned the site, it was graphically described by Mont Abbott:

> The old aborigines of these parts named us Enas-stan, after an ancient monument, the Hoar Stwun, still standing among the holly bushes at the top of Fulwell and the road to Charlbury. They stwuns, all of a yup [heap], is supposed to be the burial chamber of an ancient king, thousands of years before the Romans; and his body is fabled to have been borned from Ditchley direction all along the trail knowed for centuries as 'Dead King's Ride' or 'Dead Man's Riding'.

There is a brief contemporary description in *Oxfordshire Country Walks, No. 5, The Glyme Valley:*

> The huge standing stone, known as the Hoard Stone, would have been part of the side wall which supported a capstone as a roof. The broken remains of the other stones lie close by. The whole structure was covered with earth which has since eroded away but its size means that . . . it would have been visible over a wide area.

In the late 1990s, the Enstone Local History Circle initiated a process by which a transfer was agreed in principle making over the Hoarstone from the H. D. H. Wills 1965 Charitable Trust to the Enstone Parish Council. It appears that the Council was unable to agree to a condition that the Trust should approve the fencing of the site and require it to be maintained in perpetuity. The site is now so obscured and overgrown that no mere visitor is likely to find it.

The Fantastical Mr Bushell, Queen Henrietta's Waterworks, and Robert Southey's Cheeses

There is nothing left. As you go down the hill towards the Harrow you will see, across the Glyme, a modest house in cut Hornton stone. It was probably built out of the ruins of the grotto made there in the seventeenth century by Thomas Bushell, who began life as a youth under the protection of the great Francis Bacon, was fetching enough to attract the notice of King James I, and survived to become Master of the Mint to King Charles I. During the Commonwealth he leased the Crown Mines from the Protector.

After Bacon's death Bushell married and lived at Enstone,

> where, having some land lyeing on the hanging of a hill facing the South, at the foot whereof runnes a fine cleane streame which petrifies, and where is a pleasant Solitude; he spoke to his servant, Jack Sydenham, to gett a Labourer to cleare some Boscage which grew on the side of the Hill, and also to dig a Cavity in the hill, to sitt and read, or contemplate. The Workman had not worked an hower before he discovers not only a Rock, but a rock of an unusuall figure with Pendants like Icecles as at Wokey Hole, Somerset, which was the occasion of making that delicate Grotto and those fine Walkes.
>
> The Grotto belowe lookes just South; so that when it artificially raineth, upon the turning of a cock, you are entertained with a Rainbowe. In a very

The Wells, Enstone

little pond opposite to the rock . . . stood a Neptune, neatly cutt in wood, holding his Trident in his hand and ayming with it at a Duck which perpetually turned round with him, and a Spanniel, swimming after her . . .

Here in fine weather he would walke all night. Jack Sydenham sang rarely: so did his other servant, Mr Batty. They went very gent. in cloathes, and he loved them as his children. He did not encumber him selfe with his wife, but here enjoyed himself thus in this Paradise till the War brake out, and then retired to Lundy isle.[1]

Mr Bushell's pastoral paradise was given an airing on 23 August 1636. The King and Queen rode over from Woodstock in a cavalcade heading a procession of coaches carrying conscripted heads from Oxford colleges and other grandees. Mr Bushell introduced them to his waterworks, and the Queen 'commanded the same to be called after her own *Princely* Name, *HENRIETTA*: At which time as they were entring it, there arose a *Hermite* out of the ground, and entertain'd them with a Speech . . . Then was the Rock presented in a *Song* answered by an *Echo*, and after that a Banquet'.[2]

Nearly 250 years later, Robert Graves wrote:

> The Queen was delighted with the pleasant coolness of the grotto, but said that, looking about her, she saw nothing better to rest her eye upon than a tall, wet rock . . . Suddenly a music sounded . . . which was a signal for the keeper of the water works to turn on the brass cocks, one by one. Then, in front of the rock, first rose up a chequer hedge of water, from little pipes set at a slant, and next two stout side columns of water, making an arch . . . Then up sprang two little dancing jets of rose-coloured water, each tossing

1 From Aubrey's *Brief Lives*.
2 From Robert Plot, *Natural History of Oxfordshire*.

up a golden ball and holding it suspended at the height of about three feet.

The Queen reached forward and caught one of the balls, which was of hollow gold, and opened it and discovered a little French compliment inside and a marchpane sweetmeat . . . She prompted the King to take his ball too, and when it was opened he found in it a little portrait, painted on ivory, of the Queen . . .³

All in all, the Royal visit was a resounding success. The Queen gave Thomas 'an entire mummie from Egypt, a great raritie'. But calamity fell upon them all with the reverses of the civil war. The 'mummie' grew mouldy, the buildings decayed. Then, in 1674, the Earl of Litchfield restored them. But the real glamour had departed. The tenant of the Litchfield Arms let the place out for balls. John Jordan reports an ancient Mrs Nash as remembering 'as many as sixteen carriages and four attending on one such occasion, and on another a carriage and six, all being coal black horses'. But Jordan goes on:

> Within the last few years [he was writing in the 1850s] all remains of the waterworks and banqueting house have been demolished. For a long time the banqueting house had become a carpenter's shop . . . and the kind of cellar that enclosed the rock still existed. But about the year 1846, even these relics were ruthlessly destroyed, the banqueting house was pulled down, and its materials used to build a small house adjacent; the vaulting of the cellar thus became exposed, and fell into decay; and now at last almost the very site is swallowed up in ruins, more thick and impervious than the briars and bushes whence Thomas Bushell first emancipated the Goldwell.⁴

'All this were long before my time' said Mont Abbott. 'In my young days "Queen Henrietta's Waterworks" were the privy behind the Harrow Inn. Owen Reagan were the landlord. When a charabang party anchored there on their way to the 1924 Wembley Exhibition a snooty passenger complained about the "disgusting amenities". "It were good enough for Queen Henrietta," Owen says, "it be good enough for thee!"'

Robert Southey, the poet and biographer of Nelson, left Oxford after dinner one July day in 1805 to continue a journey through England, and stopped at Enstone 'a village where the stage would change horses at a convenient hour the next morning. We were told there were some water-works which would amuse us. It was but a melancholy sight . . . every thing about them was in a state of decay.' Southey was cheered up, however, because they brought him two sorts

---

3 From Robert Graves, *Wife To Mr Milton*.
4 Jordan described the Goldwell as 'an encrusting spring and objects left in it become covered with a deposit of limy matter'. This encrustation has a golden look to it, particularly under water, and may well account for the name of the spring. On the other hand, *golde* is Old English for 'marigold' which, compounded with w[i]elle, could mean that marsh marigolds grew there.

of cheese at supper that night at the Litchfield Arms, 'neither of which had I ever before met with; the one was spotted with green, being pleasantly flavoured with sage; the other veined with the deep red dye of the beet root: this must have been merely for ornament, for I could not perceive that the taste was in the slightest degree affected by the colouring. There was upon both cheeses the figure of a dolphin, a usual practice, for which I have never heard any reason assigned.'[5]

The Character of Thomas Bushell

Antony à Wood said some scurrilously pointed things about Thomas Bushell. 'My Lord Bacon was in disgrace, and his man Bushell having more buttons than usuall on his cloake, they sayd that his lord's breech made buttons and Bushell wore them – from whence he was called buttond Bushell.' He was, Wood continues, able to 'bewitch' and draw men into his projects so that he ruined a number. Mr Goodyere of Oxfordshire was undone by him, and Bushell was a master of the art of running into debt and died owing £120,000. He wrote, in 1628, a little confessional entitled The First Part of Youths Errors. Written by Thomas Bushel, the Superlative Prodigall and, according to himself, he had led an evil life. Nevertheless, he seems to have had considerable ability, an ingenious wit, and a fantastical eccentricity.

Adams' Stores and Naboth's Vineyard

Adams' General Stores remains after well over 100 years the hub of the village of Neat Enstone – and of Church Enstone, too, for there is no shop there – and the store was, at the end of 1998, combined with the Post Office. This was only logical in a small village. It was also historically apt, for one Adams was the Postmaster in the coaching and, later, railway days, and another was the storekeeper.

In about 1870 the shop was in what became the Litchfield Arms Inn, which belonged to Lord Dillon. The Litchfield Arms, a famous coaching inn, 'be all gone now and a posh housen-estate risen in its stead' [Mont Abbott]. But, in 1872, the School Board was required to establish a school at Neat Enstone and wished to acquire a piece of land, between where the school now stands and the Litchfield Arms, as a playground for the children and a garden for the headmaster. Lord Dillon, of Ditchley Park, to whom the ground belonged, refused to sell. The School Board was determined and referred to Whitehall. A compulsory purchase order was made.

5 From Robert Southey, *Letters from England* XXXIV.

Adams' Stores

Lord Dillon was incensed. Mr Joseph Adams was given notice to quit his premises, the Stores, as were other members of the School Board who rented houses belonging to the Ditchley Estate. Furthermore, having been frustrated by the compulsory purchase order, Lord Dillon promptly erected, on the piece of land that remained, two cottages, on which he placed a stone inscribed 'Naboth's Vineyard'. The reference is to 1 Kings XXI and means: 'They shall not take away from me my inheritance'.

Lord Dillon was remorseless. He sent Mr Adams a bill for £75 for interior repairs to the place he had been compelled to leave. Mr Adams ignored the bill.

When Joseph was displaced by the 16th Viscount, Mr Brassey of Heythrop came to the rescue. Manor Farm, in the centre of Neat Enstone, was at that time, 1890, occupied by a Mr Louch who was on the look-out for a larger farm because he had three growing boys. Mr Brassey offered him a farm at Little Tew and, at the same time, arranged with Mr Adams that, if he would take the farm, Mr Brassey would build him a shop at the end of the house that faced the street. This accounts for what now seems to be an eccentric conjunction of Manor Farm and the shop.

Lord Dillon, who controlled the 'living', was, in other words, patron of the established Church of England, and was at this time frequently confronted by Mr Adams who, for his part, was a non-conformist. A particular bone of contention was the 'Beef Charity' established under the will of Benjamin Marten (*see* section under 'St Kenelm's Church'). This was supposed to be used to provide meat for twenty poor people of the parish. It was administered by a committee that included the vicar among its number. Mr Adams said it was practically impossible for someone who was not a member of the established church to get elected to the committee. He alleged that there was discrimination in the selection of the recipients.

At the time of the trouble with Lord Dillon, another Mr Adams (John) was the local schoolmaster. He, too, was a non-conformist, and the religious factions affecting the school made things so uncomfortable that he felt compelled to resign. He eventually took over the Post Office and remained there for the rest of his life.

The Post Office then was where the road turns into Neat Enstone village as you approach from Oxford. Says Mont Abbott: 'The corner up at the top end by the Post Office were even sharper and in they days even horse traffic was forced to travel carefully. The siccy [sycamore] tree now standing free on the pavement were then enclosed deep in Johnny Adams's garden behind the wall. Mrs Adams had an old horseshoe rammed into it to anchor her washing line.'

Nearing the turn of the twentieth century, the Post Office and Stores were combined in the shop on the Green – Enstone Post Office and Adams' Stores.

Joseph Adams lived to the age of 100.[1] The last Adams to run the shop was James Alexander Adams (Alec). According to one survivor of those times, Alec 'was a shrewd old bugger. Every Saturday, after closing, he would *burn* overripe fruit and vegetables. When asked why he didn't sell them off cheap, he replied: "If I did that, they'd all hang around Saturday evenings rather than buying during the week!"'

Mr Jolly and His Ricks – A Moral Tale

The most important figure in the village towards the end of the coaching era was the coach and wagon proprietor, John Jolly. He lived

---

[1] Winifred Bennett's *Album* reports: 'A small child at Enstone School was asked to write the story of Adam and Eve. She wrote "Adam was a very old man. He lived to be 100 years and 8 months old. He died last week and was buried in Enstone churchyard."'

at Enstone House and owned land in the parish. His name is perpetuated by the name Jolly's Ricks given to a piece of land at the junction of the Bicester–Charlbury road with the Oxford road – where Worth's garage now stands. Evidently Mr Jolly accumulated a great quantity of unthreshed wheat at the time of the Crimean War (1854–56). He gambled that the price would rise because of the stoppage of supplies of wheat from Russia. But the price of wheat never rose as much as he had expected, rats infested the ricks, and eventually the cost of threshing exceeded the value of the grain produced.

John Jolly's wagons from Birmingham called at his house every Tuesday, Thursday, and Saturday; those from Worcester every Monday, Wednesday, and Saturday, and those from Stourbridge every Friday. There were similar carter services in the reverse directions.[2]

---

2 Information from *Pigot's Directory*, 1830.

Church Enstone

Before 1790 two roads came through Church Enstone, the first through the Common, past the Mill to the church. The other led from the Rectory barn, crossed the first road bearing to the left from the square, skirting Hindjones into Cling-clang Lane. That lane carried on across the present B4022 to what is now only a bridleway past Drystone Hill House, down by an ancient marker stone to Upper Cleveley – from where it carried on along what is now also a bridleway to Radford.

The Drive with Cow Parsley, Church Enstone

Back to Church Enstone, where Marshall's Lane was constructed in 1790, named for the family whose property it bisected. A Marshall family had long been landowners in the parish but it is not clear in what way Edward Marshall FSA (1815–1899), for a short time vicar of the parish, was related to them. Nevertheless, he owned the Church Enstone Marshall Estate between 1839 and 1899, and erected the spring-fed fountain in Marshall's Lane as a memorial to his wife. He was, according to a note in Winifred Bennett's *Album,* 'a generous giver of blankets and rugs to the people of Enstone'.

Five Chimneys, Church Enstone

Earlier Marshalls had worked the farm at the top of the lane (the farmhouse called Five Chimneys) between 1641 and 1792. Most of the farmland belonging to it was absorbed into the airfield in World War II.

The construction of the older cottages in Church Enstone suggests dates as early as the seventeenth century although there have been many changes – external as well as internal. For example, the core or original part of the Five Chimneys house amounts to only about one-third of the present structure. To take another instance, the Manor was refronted in 1790. Most of the cottages were originally thatched. In 1932, when one of them was destroyed by fire, all but one of the cottages in the Square were thatched. The 'Square' is to be identified only with difficulty because there is nothing square about it. Mr Kench, however, remembers that there used to be two more houses in it, so that it really was a square. One of those houses was probably the one destroyed by fire. Mr Kench's own house in the Square was once a pub called The Marshall Arms and has a large cellar.

Now the only pub in Church Enstone is The Crown Inn. This was once thatched but, between 1945 and 1955, it was re-roofed with tiles.

Forge Cottage had a blacksmith's shop at its western end, and Church Farm was a carpenter's shop before it became a private dwelling. Ivy Cottage, once thatched, was a general store.

Some years ago, a large fireplace was revealed on an upper floor of the Old Court House, and this is said to identify it as a place where the manor court was held.

In the Reverend Edward Marshall's day, the family lived in the Manor House (now two dwellings) which was not then cut off by a roadway from its garden with the two fine cedars. For the old road went up Church Street and wound around Forge Cottage and the Old School House. The Kennels and The Stables, now both dwellings, were clearly part of the Marshalls' property. Pinfolds, too, belonged to them and incorporated a shop. The Marshalls still owned Church Cottage in the 1890s, because there is a letter in the County Archives from an Oxford doctor to Edward Marshall about the well in the cottage garden. There had been an outbreak of diphtheria and the well was declared contaminated by being so close to the churchyard.

There were three additions to Church Enstone's housing stock in the nineteenth century. Albert Brassey of Heythrop built two pairs of substantial stone cottages bearing his monogram and the dates 1887 and 1889 respectively – one below The Crown Inn (Jubilee Cottages), the other pair further up in Church Street. The names of the upper pair, 'Easter' and 'Christmas', are modern and of no historical significance. The third addition is The Old Vicarage (1832),[1] by a notable architect, C. R. Cockerell (he did the Ashmolean, the Taylorian Institute, and, in Cambridge, the Fitzwilliam Museum). In 1856, G. E. Street and George Wyatt were carrying out major restoration work at St Kenelm's and, in that same year, Street designed the little Marshall fountain. The work was carried out by a memorial sculptor, Thomas Earp. Where the buildings of Neat Enstone are largely made of Cotswold grey oolite, there is, in Church Enstone, an attractive mix of Banbury ironstone. There is a scatter of newly built houses around the edges of the village but most are unobtrusive and they do not break the tranquillity of the place. Only two thatched houses remain. One of these, Pinfolds, occupies with its outbuildings the whole of a corner site, while the other, a house on the opposite corner named 'The Thatch', could hardly be roofed in any other way. Forge Cottage and Littlewick Cottage have Cotswold split stone shingles.[2] Many of the other houses are now roofed with composition tiles or blue slate.

At the bottom of Spring Hill and at the end of The Avenue (Mr Henderson's house) there was a bakehouse. The Corn Mill, which is at the bottom of the lane past The Crown Inn, had another. The mill machinery is still, save for an apple-wood cog or two, in working order. Mrs Huckin (ninety-two at the time of writing) remembers both the

---

[1] Alas, the *oldest* vicarage is long gone. There was once, writes Jordan, a Rectorial Mansion with fine grounds and ornamental terraces, fishponds, and walks. 'It is exceedingly probable that the Abbots of Winchcombe made this a residence for themselves occasionally . . .' The fishponds can be traced about 90 metres downhill from The Crown Inn.
[2] Quarried 1 mile south of Enstone at Fulwell until the beginning of the nineteenth century. See Wood-Jones, *Traditional Domestic Architecture in the Banbury Region.*

The Thatch, Church Enstone

The Mill House, Church Enstone

working mill and the bakehouse.[3] The village people would take their pies and joints to be cooked there, carrying them down in dishes carefully covered with cloths.

No bakeries, smiths, stores, or carpenters trade now in Church Enstone. Aside from the church and The Crown Inn, all the amenities are in Neat Enstone or further afield. It is tucked away from all intrusions (save distant noises) but, like all idyllic places, relies on that greatest of intruders, the private car.

By 1820 a revolution in English agriculture had resulted in the enclosure of open fields into hedged fields, so allowing for the better rotation of crops and pasture. Waste land, heath, and woodland were also enclosed on a vast scale. 'Great compact estates cultivated in large farms by leasehold tenants employing landless labourers covered more and more of the acreage of England, at the expense of various forms of petty cultivation and ownership'.[4]

Although there had been earlier enclosures, the last concerning Church Enstone was effected in 1844. The Right Hon. Viscount Dillon is shown as owning 244 acres 2 roods and 6 perches[5] of land in *'The Township of Church Enstone'* between *'The Township of Cleveley'* and *'The Enstone–Bicester Turnpike'*. The Reverend Edward Marshall is listed as owning all the land between the Little Tew Road, *'The Bicester Turnpike'*,

---

[3] Indeed, both mill and bakehouse were functioning as late as the 1960s. The Ivings family, who ran the mill, live there still. See also the section on Watermills.
[4] G. M. Trevelyan, *English Social History*, Longmans, Green & Co., 1942.
[5] 1 hectare = 2.47 acres; 1 rood = ½ acre; 1 perch = 5½ yards.

and *'The Township of Gagingwell'*. His allotment amounted to 365 acres, 2 roods, and 1 perch. It is the area now largely covered by the airfield.

Some 21 acres were allocated to *'The Vicar'* and lay directly north of Church Enstone on the northern side of the Little Tew Road. This piece of land was presumably part of the 'living' of whoever might be the vicar at the time. Further up that road on the same side, 14 acres were reserved for *'The Poor'*. There were four further small allocations, one identified as the Vicarage Glebe while another, Broad Close, belonged to Thomas Davis. A garden of 10 perches at Woodford Bridge is identified as belonging to Thomas Fawdry. Lastly, Wadham College is allotted a little over 7 acres.

Apart from the fact that virtually all the land was owned either by the Reverend Marshall or the Viscount, it is interesting to note that all the dwellings and other buildings in the village itself were owned by one or the other. Each had his public house – Dillon, The Crown and Marshall, The Marshall Arms. Church Enstone had survived into the mid-nineteenth century as a firmly controlled feudal entity.

St Kenelm and his Church

The manor of Enstone was given to Winchcombe Abbey by the Mercian king, Kenulph II, about AD 818. In the following year Kenulph's seven-year-old son Kenelm succeeded to the throne on his father's death. He was promptly murdered.

Poor St Kenelm! He had been given fair warning, as Chaucer explains in the words of the Nun's Priest's Tale:

> 'Now take St Kenelm's life which I've been reading;
> He was Kenulphus' son, the noble King
> Of Mercia. Now, St Kenelm dreamt a thing
> Shortly before they murdered him one day.
> He saw his murder in a dream, I say.
> His nurse expounded it and gave her reasons
> But as the saint was only seven years old
> All that she said about it left him cold.
> He was so holy how could visions hurt?'[1]

The murder, reports Jordan, 'was by his sister, that she might possess herself of the kingdom. The circumstances that gave rise to his imputed saintship were these. He, having been in life a pious child, and the place of his burial concealed to prevent the discovery of the

1 Nevill Coghill's modern English version.

crime, it was revealed . . . by an angel dropping upon the high altar of St Peter's at Rome a paper, on which appeared in golden letters these lines in the Saxon tongue:

> In Clent cow-pasture under a thorn,
> Of head bereft lies Kenelm, king-born.

His body was said to have been discovered by a ray of light falling upon the spot'. It was after this remarkable event that the Saxon church at Enstone was dedicated to St Kenelm.

Nothing of that remains, but Pevsner suggests that the present south aisle of about 1180 was an addition to the early church. Professor Pevsner is laconic in his description of the structure: 'The ponderous c16 W tower can be dated by contributions towards its building in wills of 1531 and 1546. These contributions cannot have been generous, as it is remarkably plain'. As to the body of the church, the whole looks simple enough though it is complicated in its parts, representing a variety of styles and dates through the intervening centuries. A major restoration was carried through by G. E. Street and George Wyatt in Jordan's time (1856), and the latter wrote 'our noble church was never before fitted up so perfectly'.

Messrs Wyatt and Street had not, however, included the roof in their renovations and, by May 1988, rainwater was pouring through in several places. A study was set up and determined that £250,000 would be needed to re-lead the roof and restore what had become a very damp edifice. Over a ten-week period a total sum of £170,000 was raised from an estimated population of 1250 persons. Substantial additional grants were made by English Heritage, The Historic Churches Preservation Trust, The Oxfordshire Historic Churches Trust, and The Lay Rector, Christ Church College, Oxford.

The project continued over eight years. The nave was completely re-covered in lead and repairs made to the tower, stone pinnacles, and clerestory windows. Then the north aisle was reroofed, and rotten and beetle-infested timbers replaced. At this time, too, repairs were made to the storm water drainage system, and this included the construction of a new soak-away to the south-west corner of the church. While this was being dug out, two old graves were discovered. The skulls of the occupants each had bullet holes through them. It seems very likely that these men had died in the course of the English civil war and they were re-interred in the grass bank by the lych gate with fitting ceremony.

Neat Enstone, March 1930

Neat Enstone, September 1999

Interior of the Rectory Barn

The South Porch of the Church. According to Murray's A Handbook For Travellers in Oxfordshire, 1894 *'By an ancient custom, christenings and weddings were always performed in the Church Porch, and women were churched there'.*

The wooden cogs of Enstone Mill

The last phase of restoration concerned the renewal of the roof carvings and claddings to the south aisle roof, with minor repairs to the windows. At this stage the roof timbers of the priest's hole (this is above the south entrance door) were found to be infested with deathwatch and with furniture beetle, and were all replaced.

Structural timbers and floorboards that dated from the Street/Wyatt restoration in 1856 had now to be replaced. There was a high level of damp in the voids beneath the floor. These spaces were lined with rough masonry of Victorian date, and it would seem that the medieval floor levels were removed during the nineteenth-century work. Indeed, the Reverend Jordan, who was vicar at the time, wrote that the floors were lowered by 18 inches. There were also a great many memorial slabs dating from the eighteenth and nineteenth centuries under the boards.

These slabs may well have been put away there very deliberately during the Victorian restoration, for the Rev. Jordan strongly disapproved of the practice of burials within the church Nevertheless, one of the forgotten memorials deserves to be perpetuated:

TO THE MEMORY
OF ABIGAIL LATE WIFE OF THE REV
M WILCOCKSON WHO DEPARTED THIS LIFE
MAY THE 19TH AD 1734 AND IN
THE 20TH YEAR OF HER AGE

BENEATH THIS STONE THERE LIES A FAITHFUL WIFE
CALLD HENCE BY DEATH WHILE IN THE SPRING OF LIFE
BEAUTY AND INNOCENCE IN HER COMBIND
AS THAT THE BODY THIS ADORN THE MIND
THOSE LOVELY VIRTUES THAT ENRICH THE SOUL
TRUTH HONESTY AND CANDOUR CROWND YE WHOLE

The church is not rich in memorials of interest but there is what Pevsner calls 'a strange monument with the effigy kneeling before his own tombstone'[2] to a certain Stevens Wisdom, who died in 1633. It is a rustic piece of work, crudely painted and curiously positioned, memorable for its own mysteriousness. But on the north wall of the nave there is a more useful memorial in the form of a tablet which reads:

Near this Pillar Lieth the body of Mr. Benjamin Marten of Radford, son of
Thomas Marten of Rowsham, Gent who besides many works of Charity in

---

[2] A deed of feoffment (No. 39) dated 1588 refers to *'Thomae Wisdom et Stefano filio suo'* (see Jordan p. 273). This Stephen Wisdom must be the worthy memorialised in St Kenelm's. The deed referred to ensured funding for the repair of the church and the relief of the poor. Stephen Wisdom died 1633.

his life gave by his last Will 120 pounds to Buy Lands the income whereof he ordered to be laid out on Meat to be distributed to Twenty Poor Parishioners of Enstone, Five of whom are to be inhabitants of Radford. He died February 4th 1715-6 aged 47 years.

Mr Marten's wishes were followed, with the first distribution of 'good Beefe' being made on Christmas Eve 1729 after the ringing of one of the church bells. Mr Benjamin Busby, the Churchwarden, officiated. The Charity continued for a further 267 years. By 1942 cash was paid in lieu of beef on 4 April. In the succeeding fifty-three years, the Charity paid out £3895 in grants. But, of course, it was a small charity and, at the end of 1998, it was sensibly merged into the larger Enstone Relief in Need Charity. The tablet remains as a reminder of one man's generosity.

The success of the campaign to raise funds for the restoration of the fabric of the church in the 1990s is some indication of the importance of an historical centrepiece to the community. The 1995 *Village Appraisal* confirmed 'the view that the continued existence of the Parish Church is, for a substantial proportion of residents, an essential feature of the secular parish area'.

The Rectory Barn

The great Tithe barn to the west of the church was built by Winchcombe Abbey. Pevsner queries its date: 'A re-set date-stone of 1382 . . . telling us that the barn was built by Walter de Wynforton, Abbott of Winchcombe, could be from an earlier building . . . The S. doorway and S. porch may be later.' To support his doubts about the date he quotes an expert in vernacular construction: Mr R. Wood Jones says that "by comparison with cruck forms in Oxfordshire the form of construction here is later than the given date by a hundred years"'.

But what Wood-Jones also observed in the article (*Oxoniensa*, vol. XXI, 1956) from which Pevsner quotes him was that 'the cruck buildings of north Oxfordshire appear to represent a regional type, which shows some interesting variations from other areas so far recorded, and the Enstone barn is particularly important as an early and outstanding example of the form'. He was writing in the 1950s, when the barn had fallen into disrepair. Its owner was concerned with its operation as a working barn rather than its conservation as an ancient monument. Mr R. T. Lattey, who lived at The Old Shop and was a founder of the Enstone Local History Circle, began a campaign to save the structure, and on his initiative a subcommittee of the Oxfordshire Archaeological Society was set up to raise funds for the barn's conservation. This involved Lattey in considerable correspondence with the Ministry of Public Buildings and Works, the Society for the Protection of Ancient Buildings, and various concerned individuals including, of course, R. Wood-Jones. Writing to Lattey in April 1961, Wood-Jones reveals that he now took a firmer view on the date of the Rectory Barn: 'I have somewhat amended and developed my views since [the article in *Oxoniensa*] . . . I am absolutely convinced now that the crucks and part of the masonry of the barn are of the 1382 date, although there has obviously been extensive rebuilding in later periods, including re-roofing'.

Lattey's campaign, begun in 1955, triumphed ten years later. A letter from the Ministry of Works in May 1956 advised him that the Ministry would put up £2800 against a contribution of £500 from the owner, that they had asked the County Council for a contribution towards the cost of a complete re-slating, and that preparation of contract documents was well advanced. The barn was made sound again.

It is a structure of six bays 72 feet by 26 feet, and it has seen some great doings in its time. In *Lifting the Latch* Mont Abbott relates:

> It were a topping barn, held the whole parish. Village feasts had been held in there for centuries . . . In 1911 it were a bit dilapidated after 529 years, but we was all too merry to notice. Memories of the old Queen's Jubilees in '87 and '97 was being swapped; and one old carter could remember the Coronation revels when, for a wager of ale, a young carter drove a wagon and three horses in and round and out of the barn in one fell sweep . . .
> They gave us kids a spiffing booze-up in 1911; four bottles of lemonade for each nipper . . . And in the evening, the grand Village Concert, winding up with a pretend King George and Queen Mary, and our Gil and another nipper as pages, solemnly bearing plush cushions with the silver paper crowns of Great Britain and all her Dominions and Empire – stuck with jujube jewels. I can still feel the deep hush of the crowning moment, and then the wild cheers and rejoicing when, as if by magic, the real church bells pealed out next door

The barn, originally built for the collection of tithes, has been used as an agricultural building all through the centuries. It is still so used and, while this limits access by the curious, there is some satisfaction in the knowledge that it is not merely a relic, or exhibit, but that it still serves its purpose after 600 years.

Chalford

Chalford, which lies westward from Broadstonehill off the A44, is spelt *Celford* in Domesday, and the latter lists it as having a mill.[1] It still has, though it is not in operation. The farm, together with farm dwellings nearby, has been upgraded.

Jordan wrote (1856), 'Charlford [*sic*] at the present time consists of two good farm residences, a mill for grinding bones and about ten cottages, besides the turnpike house'. He remarks on signs still then evident of 'ancient residences of the gentry'. The fact is that there were originally two settlements:

1 Nether Chalford: situated in a field called The Towns in 1743; divided into Near and Further Towns and Cuckoo Close by 1845; while, in 1857, a cottage was built with stone from old foundations. No buildings now remain.
2 Over Chalford: this is the site described by Jordan, now known as Old Chalford.

In 1341 Alice de Veysi, a widow, lived at Chalford with her son, John Brown. In 1415 Thomas Willicotes, of a local family, gave his estate there to Oriel College. A Bull of Pope Alexander III, concerning Winchcombe Abbey, refers to a chapel at Chalford. There were three tumuli at Chalford, two were ploughed over in Jordan's time producing 'an enormous mass of black and red ashes, and charred earth, amongst which were some small relics of burned metal'. This was spread on the field as fertilizer. The third tumulus produced no ash, but 'vast heaps of stones'. Two of these tumuli were sited in an area called Lower Disslings, and the third was opposite to them in Roundhill ground.

The side of the Glyme Valley in which the farm buildings stand was, in the Middle Ages, the site of Nether Chalford. The site on the further bank of the stream was Over Chalford, still on the southern side of the Chipping Norton road (A44). Traces can still be seen in the fields. In

---

1 The Domesday entry covers both Dean and Chalford, listing *two* mills, one at Dean and one at Chalford.

1279 there were about twenty households in the two villages. In 1996 there were nine dwellings in Old Chalford and four at Broadstonehill. The latter place, originally Broadstone, had the same population (four) in 1306.

For more about Chalford see 'Deserted Villages'.

Cleveley

~~~~◇~~~~

One mile south-east from Church Enstone on the River Glyme. It is a straggling settlement, the up-river end being Upper Cleveley and the down-river end Lower Cleveley. Both have mills and barns – converted now to dwellings – where mills are recorded in the Domesday Book of 1086.

In 1851 Jordan put the population at 228 living in forty-eight houses. In 1998 the population was eighty-four living in thirty-three houses (although empty or week-ending dwellings accounted for another five). But in earlier days Cleveley was bigger yet. Jordan noted signs remaining in his day of terraces, garden walks, and 'country houses with ornamented grounds about them' at Cleveley. 'Nor indeed is this to be wondered at . . . when it is considered that two of the highways of the vicinity passed through Cleveley. The ancient house (see below) attached to our charity lands and still standing here is constantly described in old deeds as "abutting on the King's highway to Oxford".' Indeed we can reasonably infer from a deed of 1399 (Jordan p. 207) that William and Elizabeth Newman were living there at that date. Indeed, the inhabitants of Cleveley in the fourteenth century are well documented.[1] Other than William Newman and his wife, there were John and Sibilla Sclatter, Elynor Torstan, John and Alice Paysel, Roger Gardiner, and John Fuller. There is an even earlier John the Fuller recorded in The Hundred Roll of 1278 who held the two mills at Upper and Lower Cleveley (the Enstone Mill was held at that time by Hugh the Miller). This suggests that at that date one of the Cleveley mills was a fulling mill (for more on 'fulling' see the Natural History section).

The ancient house, Brookside Cottages, is now two dwellings with modern additions and extensions. Even when Jordan wrote his history in the 1850s, he complained that it had been 'repaired, and thereby materially impaired in appearance'. The core of the house is

---

1 The old deeds give interesting indications of local alliances. There must have been a freeholding at Ditchley held by John of Ditchley in the late thirteenth century. In 1295 his widow, Margery, gave her daughter Isabell two houses in Cleveley which she (Margery) had been given on her marriage by her brother , Thomas Collona (Collins). Isabell married Jacob (James) of Taston and their daughter married John Newman – of Cleveley.

thirteenth century, and Jordan lamented that there had been 'an exceedingly good gothic arched doorway. Unfortunately, . . . when this ancient house was repaired . . . this doorway was taken down . . . and instead of its being restored again . . . the arch alone was rebuilt.'

John Kibble noted in his book, *Wychwood Forest and its Border Places* (1928), that 'in Cleveley an early doorway in what is now a cottage must have mention. A poor demented person some years ago was fastened with a chain to the floor here.' Jordan says that when the doorway was taken down the stones were used as quoins for Brookside Cottages. But they have no very substantial quoins. According to Winifred Bennett's Album, the cottages were restored between 1930 and 1940 by Miss Bruce, who reset the thirteenth-century window and doorway in the house. This indeed seems to have been the case.

In the yard of Upper Farm there is a dovecote. Wilfrid Robertson, a boys' adventure story writer[2] who lived at Upper Farm in the mid-1950s, wrote that the dovecote had once belonged to the Manor on the hilltop behind which was, he said, built in 1350 by Margaret of Ditchley 'and which has completely vanished today, though terraces can be traced'. In reality research has shown the dovecote to be of seventeenth-century origin. There were originally more than 200 nest holes at first-floor level. After the building ceased to be used as a dovecote, the lantern was removed and a plain ridged roof of Welsh slate replaced it. The first-floor level was lowered and the bottom three rows of nesting holes were blocked so that this area could be used as a granary. A bread oven was built in at ground level and was used as the local bakery, the topmost level still being reserved for doves. Not, as Robertson remarked, a very sanitary arrangement.

The Upper Farm Lake was made in 1972 by the then owner, Mr J. Arthur. He bulldozed and then proofed the water-meadow beside the Glyme, filling it from the river and from the springs already there. It has been stocked with trout from time to time but poachers and pike won the day. When Mr Arthur bought Upper Farm he and two helpers gutted the house, roof and all. Jimmy Widdowes, well remembered in Enstone, replastered the walls.

The Upper Mill and Mill House opposite the dovecote are now dwellings. They were the most important feature of Cleveley in the latter half of the nineteenth century, when the mill was owned by the Bliss family who also had other property there. Beside the Mill, water from a leat that runs down the valley at a higher level than the Glyme rejoins the river, and the mill race is now a waterfall. Across the lane,[3]

2 He is also listed in Kelly's Directory as being a poultry farmer.
3 This lane is identified in the Church Enstone Enclosure of 1844 as 'Cow Pen Lane'.

The bridlepath that was a turnpike, Cleveley

on the bank where the river skirts the lake, there are nettles and old plum trees where once small cottages used to stand.[4]

On the *cleve* or cliff above, the Old Cornbarn and Turnpike cottage stand at the fork of the road. The barn, being high and dry, was built to store grain from the mill. Mr N. Eley remembers that it was once called 'the drier' because corn would be spread out over the floor to dry. There is a small cottage tacked on to the end of the barn that was inhabited between the wars by a pedlar, Johnny Steele, who had a handcart from which he sold cottons and sewing gear. By the 1940s, the whole property was owned by Alec Adams, the last of the family to own the Enstone store. When Professor Sen[5] bought it in 1977, it had become three cottages last occupied by a Mrs Savage, Mrs Busby, and Mr Ward. Busby is one of the old Enstone names.

The Sens made alterations and the barn was sold to its present occupants in 1987 as a single dwelling. The same process went on in the adjacent Turnpike where three small cottages were converted to one. The name 'Turnpike' is apt, for the lane was once the main Oxford to Worcester road, before what is now the A44 existed, but whether the cottage actually functioned as a turnpike collection booth taking in tolls from traffic and drovers, cannot be confirmed. But these

---

4 These cottages were remembered by Mr H. Adams (b. 1885): 'At Upper Cleveley my mother acquired the mill run by Mr Goddard, also the large house on the bank facing the village occupied by Mr Lodge [Upper Farm]. An unusual feature of this house was a well inside the house. My mother also owned the row of cottages, one of which was occupied by my father's shepherd after he took the Manor Farm – Tom Busby by name.' The shepherd cottage stood near the spot now occupied by the Thames Water kiosk.

5 Professor Amartya Sen, Master of Trinity College, Cambridge and winner of the annual Nobel Prize for Economics, 1998.

are examples of what has happened to many of the older buildings in the parish: six small, no doubt inadequate, living quarters became two – even though the two house four persons.

Nearby them, a non-conformist chapel of 1871 became, in 1984, a family home. Further along the upper lane, towards Lower Cleveley, the house Greystones, originally thatched, began as two one-up and one-down farm labourers' cottages but, here again, additions (in 1951 and 1970) have transformed the amenities. An occupant of one of the original cottages, a Mrs Savage (who seems also to have lived in part of the Cornbarn at one time), was a formidable character. She was a widow who had lost an eye and wore a shade. She worked in Adams' store as a cleaner and once mentioned her distaste for the shade. Mrs Adams's father-in-law had worn a glass eye and, when he died, this was left behind. Mrs Adams hunted it out and gave it to Mrs Savage. It fitted perfectly and she wore it for the rest of her life.

Speaking of an acquaintance of his younger days, Mont Abbott observed: 'Briss hailed from Brissler, as Upper Cleveley was known in they days. Cleveley were a much bigger population then [in the 'twenties] than now, and postcards was addressed Brissler as distinct from Lower Cleveley'.

Lower Cleveley has, in fact, some more substantial buildings, most of them centred about Manor Farm. There is no record of there having been a manor of Cleveley, and the name 'Manor Farm' probably related the farm to its owners, the holders of the manor of Enstone at Winchcombe Abbey or, later, Ditchley, and was, perhaps, occupied by their agent or factor.[6]

Opposite are two barn conversions of the 1980s and Lower Cleveley Mill, where the mill stones still remain, if performing a mainly decorative function. There was once a beerhouse, The Malt Shovel, at Lower Cleveley, near the barns, but no trace of it remains. There is no doubt but that both the Cleveley mills were corn-grinding rather than fulling mills in their later centuries.

From Lower Cleveley the useful Glyme winds on to Radford, and yet another watermill.

---

6 The same may apply to Manor Farm at Enstone.

Fulwell

Fulwell

Turn off the road between Neat Enstone and Charlbury at the Hoarstone. You are passing through the fringe of the Ditchley Estate, and Fulwell, lying very privately in the valley, is very much a part of Ditchley. Indeed, until the mid-1970s it was, as the larger part of the estate still is, within the area of Spelsbury Parish Council.

In Domesday *Fulewelle* is listed as belonging to Robert D'Oilly (Sheriff of Oxfordshire and keeper of Oxford Castle). There were three villagers, two smallholders, and a mill. It changed little over the next five-and-half centuries – the Hearth-Tax figures for 1662 show two cottages, each with two fireplaces, and five cottages with one each.

Fulwell depended upon the fortunes of Ditchley, and that estate was much enlarged when Francis Lee married a great heiress, Elizabeth Pope, in 1677. It was their son who was created Earl of Litchfield and married the daughter of Charles II by Barbara, Duchess of Cleveland. The impact of the new grandeur had some small effect on Fulwell and it expanded modestly over the following two centuries so that, in May 1997, it could muster twenty-eight votes in thirteen dwellings.

Montague Archibald Abbott spent his last years at the Cottage, Biddy's Bottom, in Fulwell. He describes it vividly in Sheila Stewart's book, and makes an interesting conjecture:

> Fulwell pastures and farm buildings, grouped round the rickerd [rickyard], be that ancient you sensed on a still hazy morn the centuries of men and horses, workers on the land, that had been there before. I were only seven when the old stable, built of faggots, wattle-and-daub, with a bit of old thatch, were pulled down and rebuilt next to the chaff-house in ought-nine. They old stwun-masons, Ted Huckin, Walt and Harry Benfield from Taston, and old Joe Benfield from Gagingwell, gauged from its construction, and from details of all they structures that there were once quite an important settlement at Fulwell. Part of the barn were plastered inside like a church, with a narrow stwun-mullioned window, and another ruined foundation, properly pitched and rounded, like a bell-tower, nearby.

The old thatched cottages in Fulwell were restored in 1954, when the roofs were raised and dormer windows put in. They were then slated.

Gagingwell

Gagingwell lies on the Chipping Norton to Bicester road, a mile south of Church Enstone. The earliest mention of an inhabitant of Gagingwell is in a deed of 1339 when John Zanewyrthe of Gagingwell granted 3 acres of land in Cleveley to John the Fuller at Cleveley.

Jordan notes that, by the census of 1851, the population was seventy-six. In 1998 it numbered only twenty-five. The remains of an early cross stand on the green near the road. Jordan describes the scene: 'not far in advance of the spring or well that gives its name to the hamlet, there stands the relic of an ancient cross, having a large square basement or foundation, with three steps rising from it, and on top of them the lower portion of the stone upright, whence formerly sprang the lofty cross itself'.

In the 1890s a woman lived at Gagingwell who was reported to be a witch. Her name seems to have been forgotten, but she lived in the thatched cottage first on the right as you come from Enstone. She let her hair hang over her face, dressed in a long black coat, and carried a big stick. As if this was insufficient to justify her reputation, she would visit Adams' Stores in Enstone once a fortnight to replenish her own stocks of laudanum. Before the Poisons Act came into force, it was usual for village shops to stock medicinal drugs but, in this case, the witch from Gagingwell was clearly an addict.

In the late 1950s, the occupant of Wadham Farm House, behind the cross, Mr Slater, found an interesting cupboard that had been formed by a recess in the wall, the cupboard making a front to an ancient window recess. The window was of wood, with moulded jambs and mullions. It had never been glazed, and it seems that shutters were used.

The house on the other side of the road and slightly above it was originally cottages, one of which was the home of William Bowler, the last man in England to be hanged (at Oxford) for sheep stealing (1783). Unfortunately, he had left his footprints in the snow. George Busby published a ballad to celebrate the affair when Bowler's fate was still, evidently, a thing to be relished in retrospect:

The constable was set to work
To see where sheepstealers might lurk;
And by the snow upon the ground
The thief was traced and quickly found.

The constable to Hell Hill came,
The steward, shepherd, then by name.
They saw the footprints in the snow,
Which pointed out the way to go.

As on they went the track was clear,
To Gadgingwell, a hamlet near.
In house where William Bowler dwelt,
It seemed as if they mutton smelt.

On entering at dinner time,
Where dwelt the man charged with the crime,
What they saw before their eyes
At once made their suspicions rise . . .

                                              And so on!

For more about the origins of Gagingwell see 'Deserted Villages'.

Lidstone

There was once a monolith (now removed) at Lidstone, Leodwine's stone. The first reference to the place, in 1235, calls it *Lidenstan*. The remains of its corn mill can still be seen. Lidstone, like Cleveley, was probably included under Enstone in the Domesday entry. This allocates four mills to Enstone, and it is suggested that, of these, two are the Cleveley mills and a third is the mill at Lidstone. Lidstone mill was put out of action when Chipping Norton tapped its water.

In Jordan's day there were twenty-eight dwellings apart from the farm and the mill. Lidstone had a pub, named after the feudal grandees of Heythrop, the Shrewsbury Arms. That is now a dwelling. As at Chalford, there is a Roundhill field above the village, named after the tumulus in it. Thirty-eight voters are registered at May 1997, living in eighteen dwellings.

The site is that of a deserted or shrunken village, and that aspect of Lidstone is considered in 'Deserted Villages'.

Lidstone

Radford

Radford

Radford is listed in Domesday as having been in Earl William's holding. Earl William of Hereford, William the Conqueror's boyhood friend, was killed in 1071 and his lands were later forfeited by his son's rebellion in 1075. The mill is listed in the Domesday entry. The River Glyme, observes Jordan, 'turns no less than five mills between Chalford [at one end of the parish] and Radford [at the other]'. In the 1850s, he says, there were 'two substantial farm houses [in Radford], one of them being evidently an ancient manor house, a corn mill and about a dozen cottages'. According to the census of 1851, the population was sixty-seven, and the inhabited houses fifteen. In 1997, the population was thirty-nine in nineteen dwellings. Certainly, in the seventeenth century and earlier, the mill was a fulling mill. There is a reference in 1614: 'To this fulling mill belongeth a dwelling house, barne etc.'

Pevsner notes the Chapel of the Holy Trinity, 1841, by A. W. Pugin. The building is now divided into private residences.

The land around Radford has for many years been farmed by the Parsons family. Some barns, surplus to requirements, have now been adapted as workshops and out-of-centre offices.

Deserted and Shrunken Medieval Villages

Ancient villages have moved in the landscape and have sometimes expanded, contracted, or disappeared. The church was the focal point of the village. Many of the medieval parish churches built in the twelfth and thirteenth centuries were originally the private chapels of lords of the manor and each was sited near the manor house. The church was usually the only stone building in the village and it was frequently altered and enlarged, or even completely rebuilt, the position of the church and its accompanying graveyard remaining fixed. Though undoubtedly the finest house in the village, the manor house was, in most cases, replaced more than once before those genuine ones that survive today were built. Throughout lowland England the rest of the populace lived in single-storey homes with timber or clay walls. Eventually these came to have stone footings, but timber-frame or stone-built houses did not come into general use until the sixteenth and seventeenth centuries. Before that, most village buildings had a short life (perhaps thirty years) and were replaced regularly. In many villages the houses and their associated outbuildings occupied plots of land ranged along a central, unpaved street.

Thus, over a long period, a village might prosper and increase in area, as well as reusing its existing house sites. Alternatively, if the population decreased permanently, houses would also fall out of use and, if the contraction was severe, the village could cease to be a viable community, forcing the remaining inhabitants to go elsewhere. Abandoned houses might then be deliberately levelled to clear the land for another use, leaving only a trace in the soil. Undisturbed houses would also rot down and eventually become covered in turf leaving only faint, irregular humps. Each house site tends to show up as a rectangular platform, and the ditch bounding its plot may still be visible. The position of the central street can be seen as a long depression that had been slowly worn into the ground. House sites, and sometimes whole villages, can be mapped on the ground and, under favourable conditions of light, aerial photographs may also show up the surface irregularities, while sites on arable land may give rise to crop marks that outline walls and ditches.

There are now known to be at least 3000 such deserted medieval villages, mainly in the Midlands. The evidence for lost villages was first deduced by their disappearance from taxation records through which their often slow decline can sometimes be traced. Their final fate may not be known. Thorough archaeological investigations can not only confirm the plans of the buildings but, working down through successive occupation layers, can also tell us much about the history of the site and the lives of the inhabitants.

The sites of some deserted villages are now completely lost but, in many cases, apart from the visible village earthworks, there are the remains of the church or even an isolated church no longer surrounded by its former village. The name of the village is often preserved in the name of a present-day farm or the name of a parish. It was always assumed in the past, when the site of a deserted village was recognized for what it was, that all the inhabitants had perished in the Black Death in the mid-fourteenth century. Documentary and other evidence now shows that this was very rarely the case. The population of England in the early fourteenth century was higher than it had ever been before and all available land was under cultivation. Then the climate deteriorated, crops failed, and there was widespread starvation with many villages on marginal sites already in decline when the Black Death struck in 1348.

Undoubtedly, the impact of the Black Death was profound, and the social changes and altered patterns of farming that followed over the next 100 years were the main causes of the desertion of villages. With fewer people available to work the land, the survivors were able at last to demand wages for their labour, which had previously been given free to the feudal lord of the manor in return for land that the labourers could cultivate for themselves. In the Cotswolds, as in other areas, the landlords side-stepped the issue by clearing the people out of failing villages and turning arable land over to sheep pastures (called 'grounds') for wool production which needed far fewer workers and was also a valuable source of cash. In other cases the inhabitants moved out voluntarily to resettle in depleted villages on better agricultural land. This process was hastened by land enclosure in which the fragmented land holdings under the open field system, along with much common land, were consolidated (a process not finally completed in Enstone until the 1840s).

The authority on Oxfordshire's deserted villages is the book by Allison, Beresford, and Hurst, from which much of the information given here is quoted. They define a 'deserted village' as having not more than one farm, one manor house, and one parsonage left. A 'shrunken village' is one with up to six houses remaining and neighbouring earthworks of abandoned houses and streets.

By these standards the parish of Enstone contains the sites of three known deserted medieval villages: Over Chalford, Nether Chalford, and Upper Chalford or Broadstone, all close together in the upper valley of the River Glyme. On the boundary is Ditchley, close to, or under, the house of Ditchley Park. There are two more well-known examples nearby: Asterleigh, 0.5 km east of the old parish boundary by Asterleigh Farm; and Coat (or Cote) 2 km south-west of the parish to the south of Spelsbury and Taston. In addition, all the townships except Church Enstone have distinct signs of abandoned buildings in or very near to them. Detailed historical and archaeological study would be needed to distinguish between genuine shrinking of the settlement and buildings left behind as the rest of the community built new houses on other sites. The National Grid reference is given for each site mentioned to allow anyone interested to visit the area. All the sites, however, are on private land but most have roads or public footpaths passing close by.

1 *Over Chalford* (SP 344257)

The village lay on the present site of Old Chalford Farm and the remains of the water-mill; the earthworks are not easily seen though the farm can be reached on bridle paths from both sides of the valley. There were eighteen tenants in the survey of landholders made by King Edward I in 1279, the first since Domesday two centuries earlier. It was still there in 1316 but, by 1480, it was let as pasture by the new owner, Oriel College, Oxford, so was probably depopulated during the fifteenth century.

2 *Nether Chalford* (SP 347254)

A plan of this Scheduled Ancient Monument is shown here. The origins of the village are unknown but it was traditionally taxed with neighbouring Over Chalford. By 1743 the sloping pasture on which the

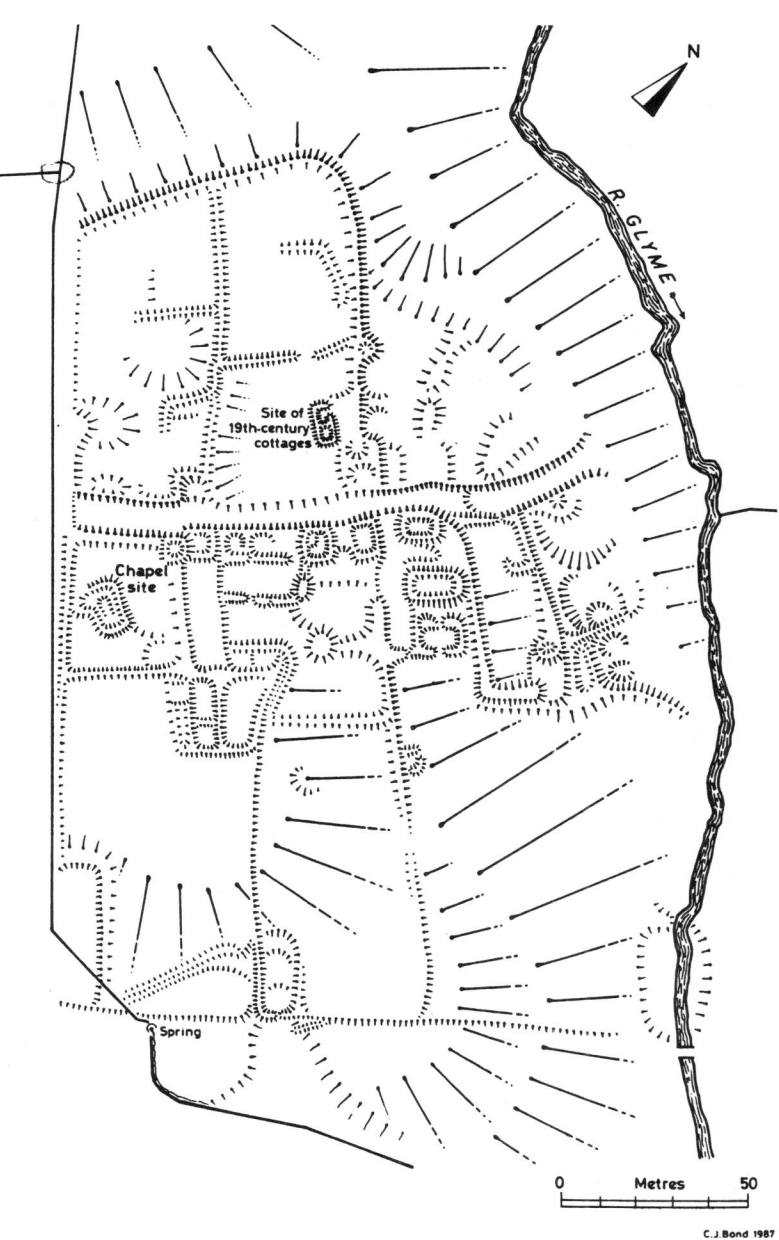

Settlement Earthworks – Nether Chalford, by C. J. Bond

site lies was known as 'The Towns'. The layout of street and houses is exceptionally clear, and the site of the chapel has been located. The stones of wall footings project above the turf in some places. Two cottages were built with salvaged stone in the mid-eighteenth century but these, too, are now in ruins. Bond (1989) considered that there is possible evidence of an even earlier settlement on the site. The site can be seen from the bridle path running south-east to north-west from Lidstone.

3 *Upper Chalford or Broadstone* (SP 353252)

The layout of this Scheduled Ancient Monument is very well preserved. It can be seen across the valley from the bridle path passing Nether Chalford. This path is said by Jordan to have been the former highway before the turnpike road was made that ultimately became the modern A44. Broadstone Hill Farm now lies more than 1 km to the north.

The early history is similar to that of Nether Chalford but it had probably ceased to exist as a settlement by the time of the Black Death. Later references to the site are confusing, although it is known to have belonged to Cold Norton Priory and later to have been leased to King Henry VIII.

4 *Ditchley* (SP 390211)

Knowledge of the existence of this village is based almost entirely on documentary evidence. The site itself is mostly covered by the present mansion and its adjacent buildings but possible traces of walls have been found. There was, however, a village recorded by 1295, and it continued in existence until at least 1665 when there was only one remaining household on which the Hearth Tax was levied. Possible traces of walls have been found. The name refers to the prehistoric Grim's Ditch nearby.

5 *Asterleigh* (SP 400224)

The name of this village is preserved in the farm on the site and in the name of the parish of Kiddington-with-Asterleigh. The site has been partly destroyed by quarrying and is no longer visible from the public footpath close to its southern edge. It started as a small village with only four taxable tenants in 1306, and there was a church of which the site is known. By 1466 the parish of Asterleigh became so reduced through poverty, depopulation, and epidemics that it was joined to Kiddington.

6 *Coat* (SP 355214)

A detailed map is given by Bond (1989) showing farmhouses in which, unusually, the animal accommodation and barns were separated from the main houses. The name lives on in nearby Coathouse Farm. It was in existence in the thirteenth century when it belonged to the Abbey of Eynsham which did not collect any rents after 1350. It seems likely, therefore that the whole population died from the Black Death or, if there were survivors, that they were forced to leave.

The following are the more obvious examples of village shrinkage, or perhaps gradual movement, in our parish. Several were noted by Jordan in 1857 though he tended to interpret house platforms as 'garden terraces', and took them as evidence of a former mansion on the site. There will also have been many cases of sites being re-used, Some are documented, as in the case of the Old Vicarage in Church Enstone which was built in 1836 on the site of an earlier one.

1 *Cleveley* (SP 391239)

House platforms and occasional stones protruding through the turf can be seen from the bridle path crossing Bissel's Close between Greystones and Manor farm.

2 *Enstone* (SP 377244)

The field known as Rod's Close (bounded by the loop of Chapel Lane) has at least one house platform and a hollow way running north–south that are visible from the road when the light is low. On the northern side, there are also the remains of buildings, such as a wheelwright's workshop, that have gone out of use within living memory.

3 *Fulwell* (SP 380232)

Walking from Fulwell towards Cleveley along the old carriage road, on the south side of the present hamlet house platforms and a big hollow way are plain to see on the sloping ground to the north. The County Sites and Monument Record quotes a Mr Henderson of Enstone Local

History Circle in 1970 as pointing these out and mentioning 'a local tradition of a larger hamlet near here'. The writer has picked up fragments of thirteenth to fifteenth-century pottery from beside the path.

4 *Gagingwell* (SP 407252)

An area of several hectares of obvious lumps and bumps can be seen from the Enstone to Bicester road in the corner of the field where the road turns sharply northwards beside Abbey Farm. There is a further view from the bridle path running down the western side of the same field. More earthworks are visible on the south side of the road. Jordan was aware of them 140 years ago and says the main site was known as 'the gardens'. He also states that a small field nearby was a vineyard and launches into a three-page lecture on wine!

5 *Radford* (SP 409241)

There is a small patch of distinct earthworks on the top of the hill in the field opposite the farmhouse of Radford Farm. Local tradition holds these to be the remains of abbey buildings. Jordan, however, discussed this site at length in 1857, and had been unable, despite an exhaustive search in the Bodleian Library in Oxford, to find any record of a religious house on the site, apart from its name of Chapel Close. He concluded that there had been property in the area (perhaps a grange or abbey farm) belonging to a religious body, and that a small church or chapel had once stood here, of which the remains were, and still are, visible.

At the present time villages throughout Oxfordshire are expanding even though constrained by planning regulations. This expansion is quite different from that in the past which would have reflected local rural prosperity. For most of the twentieth century there has been a steady migration of people from the country to the towns. There is also a greatly diminished need for agricultural workers as farms have become mechanized and techniques have changed. Aerial photographs of Enstone show some of the many houses that have been built since 1930 but do not reveal how their inhabitants have changed; many houses are now occupied by people who do not work in the parish. Neither do they pinpoint buildings such as barns, stables, forges, or the local shops and other redundant buildings that have now been converted into houses.

Water-mills

Water-mills and windmills were intended primarily for grinding corn. Water-mills were introduced into Britain by the Romans who had used them for this purpose since the first century BC. Windmills appeared only in the twelfth century AD and are more commonly found in eastern areas.

In 1983 Wilfred Foreman listed the remains of six water-mills in the parish of Enstone of which the last to have worked was the one at Church Enstone in the 1960s. It is interesting that at least three mills (Church Enstone, Lidstone, and Radford) were also linked with baking and had bread ovens and bread-making equipment on the premises. Two others (Cleveley Lower Mill and Radford) were mentioned as fulling mills involved in cloth production in the Middle Ages but later switched to corn. The mill at Old Chalford was rebuilt as a bone mill to grind fertilizer before it finally went out of use. In its final form Lidstone had the biggest wheel in the county.

The leat of the mill at Upper Cleveley is still in good repair and normally carries part of the flow of the river from Woodford Bridge down to Cleveley where it discharges beside the mill buildings as a waterfall. Below this point, dredging operations in the river in 1996

Cleveley: the line of the fence follows the line of the leat to the Mill

brought up a quantity of late twelfth- or early thirteenth-century potshards of locally made coarseware cooking pots.

Henestan (Enstone) is given in Domesday as having four water-mills (assessed at 19 shillings), presumably on the same sites as the later ones. Indeed, because the Romans farmed here, they could well have built the first mills.

Windmills were less of a feature in Oxfordshire and, though none is known for our parish, Foreman listed three old sites close by. The most important was a well-documented nineteenth-century post mill south-east of Chipping Norton, only 1.5 kilometres away.

Foreman also listed the names of all the millers he could find recorded in Oxfordshire up until the time of the county directories. His list includes: Slaemaker, Cleveley, 1664; Richard Hartley, Enstone, 1734; Wm Goodrich, Lidstone, 1819; John Lister, Radford, 1827.

The Naming of Places

Enstone

Enna's stone, says Ekwall *(Concise Dictionary of English Place-Names).* Gelling *(The Place-Names of Oxfordshire)* agrees, adding: 'the names Lidstone and Enstone are composed of a personal name and the element *stan* (or stone)'. It is spelt *Henestan* in the Domesday Book.

But the Reverend John Jordan, Enstone's vicar in the 1850s, is very firm about *giants:* 'as the termination is of Saxon origin, so no doubt is the first part of the word also . . . a word expressive of the hugeness of the stone, or of its supposed primitive erectors. The word is the Saxon *ent,* signifying a giant.' Enstone, he says, derives its name from the *Entastan,* the Giant's stone.

The prefix 'Church' as in Church Enstone needs no clarification. Neat Enstone is first recorded in 1300 as Net Enestan. In 1379 it becomes Netenestane, in 1413 Netenstane, and in 1599 Nettenstogn. The first element may be Old English neat, meaning cattle. Neat Enstone would seem, from the date of its earliest reference, to be of later origin than Church Enstone and, having no church of its own, to have been in the parish of Church Enstone. Neat Enstone became important, however, as a posting station, for changing horses etc. on the high road from Oxford to Birmingham and Worcester until the railways (temporarily) took away the road traffic. In the coaching days, Neat Enstone had six inns, and it was in those days that it acquired a new alternative name: Road Enstone.

Nigel Hammond *(The Oxfordshire Village Book)* is non-committal about the meaning of Enstone: 'the place name may derive from the Giant's Stone or Hoar Stone on the south of the village or perhaps from the ancient name of the Glyme, namely the Enis'. The only other person to call the Glyme the Enis was Edward Marshall, and he produced no evidence to justify it.

The River Glyme

The river is Glim in the Cartularium Saxonicum of 1042, and means 'Bright Stream' says Ekwall, adding that it is difficult to say if the name is English or Celtic. If English, it is related to 'gleam'.

Broadstonehill

Gelling writes: 'second element stan (stone). There is a monolith about half a mile away. The first element could be either the personal name Brada or the adjective brad, broad: the former is perhaps more probable.'

Chalford

Spelt Celford in the Domesday Book. Ekwall says the name means 'chalk ford', that is a ford where limestone was carried across or where limestone was found.

Cleveley

Gelling defines the name as meaning a wood or clearing on a cliff, where 'cliff' may mean 'river bank' or 'hillslope'. The 'ley' element is the Old English leah, which corresponds, says Ekwall, to Old High German loh 'grove', Old Norse lo 'low-lying meadow'. It is this last definition that best suits the 'ley' in Cleveley.

Fulwell

The name means 'dirty stream'. Old English Fūl, 'dirty' appears in a number of Oxfordshire stream names and has a similar meaning in Fulwell, near Mixbury, or Fulbrook, near Burford. Was it dirty with fuller's earth?

Gagingwell

Variously spelt in medieval documents, Gadelingwelle being fairly representative. Ekwall took the first element, gaedeling, to be Old English for 'kinsman, relative' and the second from wella, 'spring'. Gelling points out 'This word is recorded in Middle English, however, as a term of reproach, and later, in the 16th century, with the meaning of "wanderer, vagabond"'. The earliest mention of an inhabitant of Gagingwell is in a deed of 1339, when John Zanewyrthe of Gagingwell granted 3 acres of land in Cleveley to John the Fuller of Cleveley.

Lidstone

There is a difference of opinion between Ekwall and Gelling as to the meaning of this place-name. Gelling defines it as 'Leodwine's stone', adding 'Ekwall considers that this name contains the parish name Enstone with a distinguishing prefix. But there is a monolith at Lidstone as well as one at Enstone, and another quite near to *Broadstone Hill*. It seems reasonable, therefore, to interpret the three names separately as having only the element "stan" in common.'

Radford

That the name means 'riding-ford', the ford that can be crossed on horseback, from Old English rad, 'riding' is suggested by Ekwall and by Gelling. This distinguishes Radford, Oxfordshire from other Radfords where 'red ford', the soil being red near the ford, is a likelier interpretation.

The Naming of Persons

◇ ◇ ◆ ◇ ◇

A Review of Enstone, published in 1971 by the Parish Council, talks of Jack Claridge who was a local character and expert poacher earlier in the century. He lived near the Alley by the Green at Neat Enstone. Aside from poaching he was a rat catcher, and the 'Review' describes how he kept a supply of live rats at home and took regular sackfuls of them by carrier's cart to Oxford. He would sell them to undergraduates for rat-killing competitions. Terriers were loosed to kill the rats, and bets placed on the dogs.

Life might have been very different for Mr Claridge had the Reverend John Jordan been more successful in his researches half a century earlier. Jordan reports that a wealthy Quaker from Philadelphia, Samuel Claridge, had been shipwrecked on a voyage to England and died, unmarried and intestate. 'There are still persons' wrote Jordan, whom the Claridges had approached, 'conceiving themselves to be the rightful heirs of this property, but unable to find the necessary proof of their being so . . .' He could not, in the end, make a satisfactory connection.

There is a handful of names that have been well known in Enstone over the generations. Many families, such as the Venvells, the Claridges, the Hawkins, and the Sheffields, are chronicled in *Lifting the Latch*. Some are gone and some are in their last generation locally. Some are landmark names: Charles Sheffield won the *Croix de Guerre* in World War II and was mentioned in Despatches. William Herbert was an anti-aircraft gunner on convoys to Murmansk and Malta, receiving a Russian medal for the first as well as British medals for both.[1]

Messrs Huckins, Hawtins, and Newman were among the Old Contemptibles of World War I. Still further back, William Sheffield recalled (1951) celebrating the relief of Mafeking under the old elm that once stood on the green. In 1962, at the age of 86, Jim Ivings remembered ploughing with four oxen as a ten-year-old in Cleveley

---

1 His Russian medal is inscribed in Russian, 'Forty Years of Victory in The Great Patriotic War 1941–45', and he received it in 1985. The Convoys to Murmansk and to Malta incurred horrific losses in ships and men. Charles Sheffield died in August 1999.

fields. Mont Abbott declared that 'Jim Ivings were the last in Enstone within living memory to plough with oxen'.[2] Four Enstone names are listed here, together with some evidence of their persistence through the centuries. 'Directory' refers to the number of subscribers listed under a name in the Residential Section of *The Phone Book: Banbury and District:*

Slatter

Mentioned first in 1345, again in 1750 in the parish records. It is, says Jordan, 'a common name in the parish even to the present time' [1856]. There are twenty-two entries in the Directory. The nearest Slatters to Enstone now are in Chadlington.

Wakefield

First mentioned in the parochial registers in 1575, again in 1757. There are twelve entries in the Directory. A family still resident in the parish.

Busby

First mentioned in a deed of 1588, again in the parochial register for 1661. Still alive and kicking (Quarry Close) in 1999. Twenty-six entries in the Directory.

Newman

This is not an uncommon name in the country as a whole; nevertheless, eighty-four entries in the Directory suggests that a local habitation accounts for some of these. William Newman of Cleveley appears in documents of 1346. There are further instances in 1664, 1698, and 1711. Mont Abbott recalled a carter called Newman in Enstone during World War I.

---

2 A farmer named Kench, who had 1000 acres in the district, worked five teams of oxen, finding them more economical in use than horses. The names of the oxen in Jim Iving's team were: Colonel, Captain, Dumpling (a bull), and Traveller.

Ladies Bountiful

The tradition of manorial patronage carried on well into the first half of the twentieth century. But perhaps because of the historical dominance of Winchcombe Abbey and because Ditchley was so great as to be semi-detached from the more intimate concerns of the parish, Enstone and its satellite 'towns' became subject to the attentions not of a singular patron but of several.

There was, for example, Mrs Brassey, the wife of Albert Brassey at Heythrop. According to Mont Abbott, reminiscing years later, Mr Brassey's horses 'were massive Cleveland bays, all to match; and his coaches, carriages, broughams, wagons, was all decked out in the Brassey colours'. In February 1883, the Deanery Magazine, up-to-date as ever, reported:

> On the Saturday before Christmas the schoolroom was filled with red cloaks, blue cloth capes, serge dresses, shawls, flannel, linen, blankets etc., which Mrs Brassey kindly gave as Christmas presents to the boys and girls in the day and Sunday school and to the mothers in each house on the estate. Unfortunately Mrs Brassey was unable to give them away in person, as she had met with an accident in the hunting field the day before. Fraulein Hecht, assisted by Misses Lily, Rose and May Brassey, dispersed the acceptable and useful gifts (Connemara cloaks).
>
> On Saturday Dec 30th Mr and Mrs Brassey kindly entertained all the schoolchildren in the hall, after which they saw that grand old favourite – a Punch and Judy show to the great delight of both parents and children.

Viscountess Dillon, whose husband became irascible in his later years, seems to have been a gentle person appropriately memorialized by the pretty gothic fountain put up by her children at Taston. Her son, Harold, was the last of the Dillons to live at Ditchley. Horace Adams remembers Viscountess Dillon calling on his mother in about 1890: 'travelling in a carriage and pair, the coachman and attendant arrayed in the cockaded hats of those days. Her Ladyship often brought my mother presents on her birthday and presented her with a five pound note when I was born.'

In Mont Abbott's own day, Miss Dillon took an interest in the Enstone Women's Institute. She 'and others of high-born rank, who'd kept theyselves uppity on their high horse before the [1914] war, now seemed more natural'. By the time the next war came along Mrs Ronald Tree was the doyenne at Ditchley, organizing a canteen for the Company of the 8th Battalion Durham Light Infantry based at Enstone.

Between wars there was Miss Bruce – 'or "Miss Brusque" as some called her' says Mont Abbott. It was she who built Drystone Hill House above Cleveley and alongside the footpath where it crosses the Tews road to carry on as Cling-Clang Lane. Mont Abbott again: 'Not only her own house were kept in order but other folks' affairs as well . . . Her were generous too. It were her as drove away the final debt for the new Parish Hall. The whole village was kept on the right track with Miss Bruce in her helmet and goggles firmly handling the early twenties in her open racing Amilcar.'

Tales from Horace

The late Horace Adams, who was born in Enstone in 1885, wrote down in 1961 his recollections of boyhood. He had been sent to boarding school at Banbury at the age of nine, and stayed there until he was sixteen, so that most of his memories concern the period up to 1894 and over school holidays between 1894 and 1901. They are remarkably vivid. Here are two tales and a description of the postal service at the beginning of the twentieth century:

Patience Taplin and the Mice

Patience Taplin next door, a widow living alone was a great character. She was always at work, turning the swathes of hay in a white sun bonnet in the early summer, twisting straw bonds, and tying up the sheaves of corn, and later helping lift the root crops. In the winter she was in great demand when thrashing took place. I have seen corn being thrashed in a barn by means of the hand flail; but the portable steam engine drawn by two to four horses according to the road-gradients and a threshing machine let out by one or two of the large farmers were in common use. Her job when threshing took place was on the machine cutting the bonds of the sheaves and passing the loose sheaves to the machine feeder. Particularly after a wet summer the ricks were left some considerable time before threshing to enable the corn to become well dried, so that they were often infested with rats and mice. On the removal of the thatch the rats usually quickly worked down to the rick bottom, but many of the mice remained in the sheaves before the bonds were cut. Patience always wore voluminous petticoats with the result that the mice often sought refuge about her person. She did not seem to mind in the slightest. It was amazing how the village cats got to know the sound of the threshing machine and quite a number collected to feast on the mice. It was usual to have a break at

Note: *The hand flail:* two short sticks, the handstaff, and the swingle, attached to one another by a strong band of gut. The wheat is strewn on the floor. The handstaff is held in both hands, and swung over the head so that the swingle is brought down horizontally on to the heads of the ripe corn.

10 o'clock and she would descend from the top of the machine, stand in the rickyard, and shake the mice from her clothing surrounded by cats. This was repeated at the dinner break and again at knocking off time before going home. On the way home [just across the road] she was followed by the cats still capable of consuming further mice and often joined by other cats. On arriving home she would divest herself of her clothing, releasing those mice she had been unable to release before. I am aware that many would say I was romancing by recording this but I can assure those that I have witnessed this performance by the good lady on many occasions, excluding of course the latter performance in her outhouse.

How to Catch a Hare

Led by Harry Dean, who was my father's shepherd for many years, until he eventually became a keeper himself on the Ditchley estate, we were initiated into every method in the illicit capture of game. Harry would spot a bird or a hare at a great distance and if conditions were right would manage to work his way round upwind to get it. I have seen him spot a hare in a form at a distance of 100 yards or over. He would then circle round it to make sure in which direction it was facing, usually against the wind. He would then place his shepherd's crook upright in the ground facing the hare at a safe distance on which he hung his coat. He would then walk away and take a long detour to the rear of the hare against the wind and finally fling himself upon the hare from behind – his theory being that the coat, having been placed at such a distance in front of the hare so as not to disturb it, and yet be in the sight of his victim, it would be watched by the hare as the possible cause of trouble, quite unaware of Harry's approach from the rear.

Catching the Post

Enstone in those days was quite an important postal centre, feeding a wide area. A night mail van drawn by two horses or more according to the road and weather conditions would start from Chipping Norton every evening, arriving at Enstone at 9.25 p.m. So punctual was its arrival in the village that people set their clocks accordingly. At exactly 9.30, the mail having been handed over, the signal was given for departure by the postmaster who received mail up to 9.15 p.m. The van then picked up mail at Kiddington and Glympton and on to Woodstock, where horses were changed. From there mail was collected and delivered to Oxford, arriving soon after midnight. The return journey was then made when incoming mail had been sorted. It was put down at Enstone very early in the morning, so that letters and parcels were delivered in the village from 7 a.m. onwards. It was very rarely the mail failed to arrive in reasonable time, and letters posted up to 9.15 p.m. were delivered in London by the first post next morning – the same applying in the opposite direction.

The *Enstone Ensign*

Enstone and Heythrop parishes are served by an informative local news and information service in the shape of a monthly newsletter called the *Enstone Ensign*.

The *Ensign* grew from an initiative developed by a Stewardship Committee set up by the then Vicar in 1984. The aim was to mobilize the talent thought to be available locally in the service of the community as a whole. The idea was that a more general involvement of people in community affairs would also lead to an increased commitment to providing funds for the conservation of the church – which has proved to be the case.

The Committee set up ten groups of about ten persons to discuss and propose ideas. The groups met one evening a week for about six weeks from September into November 1984. Their conclusions were collated into a Parish Plan, and this was presented to the public and discussed at a meeting in December of that year.

One of the proposals that emerged was that there should be a parish newsletter. Its masthead title has a naval ring to it – *Enstone Ensign* – but evidently *Ensign* was chosen simply because of its euphony with *Enstone*, and had nothing to do with the fact that the Chairman of the Stewardship Committee, Captain Foster, was a retired naval officer.

Initially the Ensign was financed by the parochial council as sponsor with voluntary donations of £1.00 a year from households, of which there were 450. It would be distributed by about fifteen volunteers, mostly churchgoers and, in due course, revenue would be raised by including advertisements. The editor, Mr Colin Wright, brought out his first issue in mid-February 1985. Ill-health obliged him to give up the editorship in 1989, when this was undertaken by Mrs Andrea Bates. The editor's husband, Mr David Bates, took on the responsibility of Advertising Agent. Those two, Mrs Coles, and the PCC's Treasurer and Secretary, Mr Henderson, have, with Captain Foster, formed a steering committee. Apart from the parochial church council, there are, at the millennium, three local company sponsors, and getting on for twenty advertisers. The Ensign has never missed an issue. It has always steered clear of anything overtly political or touching upon personalities, and increasingly includes items of historical and sociological interest to Enstonians.

The Early History of Enstone

The landscape is slowly but steadily changing. Evidence of the past surrounds us though it is being lost all the time in a continuous cycle of destruction and rebuilding. Enstone lies in an area that has been under human occupation since the end of the last ice age, 10,000 years ago. Thus, primeval woodlands on the lighter soils on the limestone hills were gradually cleared and the land farmed, yet some reverted to scrub a few centuries later; other arable land was later turned into pasture, and, at certain times, pasture has been put under the plough. The heavier soils in the valley bottoms, which were also liable to flood, could have been used only as pasture. There are many springs that emerge from the ground on slopes where porous limestone overlies impervious clay. They would have been more conspicuous before the introduction of land drainage, and a good water supply was an important factor in choosing a site for settlement.

At the parish level, the archaeological features described below show no marked grouping, except that there seem to be rather more from all periods on the south-west facing slopes to the north of Church Enstone. More arrowheads and other artefacts have been recorded there than elsewhere, many collected by Colin Edgington when he farmed in that area.

Boundaries have been marked with ditches and banks, hedges, fences, and walls according to the needs of the time and the methods available, though usually traces remain after abandonment. Buildings, too, are constantly being altered or replaced; important ones – such as churches – often stand over the remains of earlier structures. Others gradually crumble until they have all but disappeared into the soil where, nevertheless, they can still be traced. Footpaths, tracks, and roads also persist for very long periods, though their size and function may change and some eventually vanish.

The outlines of buried walls and refilled ditches can be seen in aerial photographs of growing crops as 'crop marks', and many have been recorded for Enstone. Slight changes in the surface, visible in low sunlight or light snowfall, can also betray the presence of underlying structures, most notably in the case of the Roman villa at Ditchley, first detected in this way, and the deserted medieval villages in the upper Glyme valley.

Apart from buildings, the most useful finds for archaeological study are stone artefacts which last virtually for ever. Pottery fragments (shards) also persist for thousands of years, though they become broken up and worn in soil that is repeatedly cultivated. Bones also last for very long periods in suitable soils (human burials are extremely important sources of information about the culture from which they came).

Objects of bronze or iron survive less well but are nevertheless important; jewellery and coins are also invaluable because they can often be precisely dated and tell us much else besides. All this sort of material is constantly coming to light, but virtually nothing was recorded before the nineteenth century, and even today a lot of small finds are not reported.

The parish of Enstone itself has existed as an entity for less than 900 years. When Domesday was compiled in 1086 there was a Saxon manor called Henestan that derived its name from the Hoarstone (see 'The Naming of Places'). The national system of organized parishes came a little later. In considering our early history it makes sense, therefore, to look beyond the exact boundary of today; even that has been in place for only twenty years.

Palaeolithic, Mesolithic, and Neolithic Periods

Over the last 700,000 years, north-western Europe has experienced alternating ice ages and warmer periods. For all but the last 11,000 years in this vast span of time, various palaeolithic (Old Stone Age) peoples roamed the area following a simple existence as hunter-gatherers using, among other things, stone (often flint) tools.

It is not clear when the first humans set foot in the parish. Our earliest proven inhabitants were mesolithic (Middle Stone Age) people who flourished from about 9000–4500 BC. They were still using flint tools and weapons but these were made with increasing skill and included finely shaped arrowheads and small cutting tools (microliths), leaving characteristic flakes of waste flint, especially numerous on living sites. Although there is only one official record (an arrowhead) in our parish, there is abundant evidence of mesolithic habitation in southern England. It is not difficult to find mesolithic flint fragments from tool-making and discarded tools exposed on the surface of the soil in freshly tilled fields throughout the parish. In fact, because flints come from chalk and the nearest source is many miles away, it is likely that any piece of flint picked up here arrived through human agency at some time in the distant past.

By about 4500 BC the neolithic (New Stone Age) culture was beginning to emerge, and operated for the next 2500 years. Stone was used with increasing sophistication for polished tools and leaf-shaped arrowheads, and simple pottery was made. This period saw the first agriculture, with large-scale tree clearance to grow crops and the appearance of domesticated farm animals. These things imply settlements but most living sites have long since been obliterated by later inhabitants.

The distinctive feature of the Neolithic Period is the huge monuments that were built. Strong social organization would have enabled the neolithic people to build their large ceremonial structures (henges) of stone and wood, and to prepare the long barrows in which they buried some of their dead. Our nearest example of the former is the stone circle of the King's Men near Little Rollright. Fully intact examples of long barrows, now rare, are conspicuous landmarks up to 50 metres long. Each contains a small burial chamber with one or more compartments built of massive rock slabs covered by a mound of earth. In other cases, however, the mound has now gone to expose the interior megaliths in varying degrees of disarray, as seen in our own Hoarstone and also the Whispering Knights, close to the King's Men. The Cotswolds are particularly rich in long barrows, and the name 'Hoarstone' occurs no less than eight times. Though most long barrows have now been destroyed by agricultural activity some sites are still discernible as crop marks.

Returning to the Enstone Hoarstone, it is the exposed single burial chamber of a long barrow, and would perhaps have included a portico of which nothing is now visible. The three stones still remaining upright form part of an obvious burial chamber (which, typically, faces east); the displaced capstone now lies almost buried on the north side. An article in *The Gentleman's Magazine* of 1824, illustrated with a woodcut showing a fourth standing stone, also mentions that there was a low mound. Another nineteenth-century drawing also shows the site before the present holly trees were planted. Sir Henry Dryden measured the stones in 1897, made a small excavation between the fallen stones, and found fragments of Roman pottery and coins. It is now realized that prehistoric monuments were often in use for hundreds of years and then continued to be respected long after the culture that created them had gone. It is not surprising, therefore, to find traces of Roman activity, especially as we are in an area much used in Roman times, though humbling to realize that this monument was by then already more than 2000 years old. It has been equated with other long barrows at Spelsbury, Langley, Steeple Aston and Ascott-under-Wychwood. The Hawkstone, a monolith standing in open fields less than 1 kilometre into Spelsbury Parish, has also been cited as the sole remnant of another denuded neolithic burial chamber.

The Hoarstone stands at a present-day crossroads; eighteenth-century maps, however, show an additional road running westwards to Chalford Green on the Saltway (or Green Lane). The first kilometre has reverted to arable land but the next kilometre is a farm track/field boundary, finally regaining its status as a road at the sharp corner where the present road from Lidstone to Chalford Green turns west.

In 1957, Humphrey Case reported that a deep trench cut to the west and north of the Hoarstone for pipework from the adjacent reservoir showed no sign of neolithic activity. He concluded, on this entirely negative evidence, that the twin ditches that would have been dug to provide the material for the mound must have run southwards, meaning that the burial chamber was located at the north-eastern corner of its mound.

Enstone also has two other possible long barrows. Eight slabs of rock were removed from the ground at Lidstone Market Garden after being struck by a bulldozer during work in 1970. Another site, showing as a crop mark, is located close to the headwaters of the River Glyme at Old Chalford. There are three records of neolithic flint arrowheads and three of various implements found in the parish. There must have been many other finds over the last 4000 to 5000 years, and undoubtedly more still to come!

Bronze Age

Bronze Age culture is characterized by the building of round barrows, but this period is not well marked. At the end of the Neolithic Period, stone and bronze were used in parallel for hundreds of years. Arrows were tipped with finely made barbed flint points. One has been found in Enstone 1 kilometre north of the church.

Bronze was an expensive material. None of its constituents (tin, copper, and lead) occurred locally; all had to be extracted from their ores, and the refined metals, melted together to give bronze, would then have been brought here. It was used mainly for tools, weapons, and small cast objects. Old bronze was not discarded (except in rituals) but melted down and used again. Thus, there is much less of it around than might be expected, and no bronze objects are yet known from Enstone.

Round barrows, marking single burials, form the clearest evidence of Bronze Age occupation. It was a favourite activity of nineteenth-century antiquaries to dig into them seeking the grave goods. Many barrows still survive, though often reduced to slight mounds; the more prominent are marked on maps as 'tumuli'. Many more, now ploughed out, are visible only as crop marks, called ring ditches, which show where the earth was dug out to form the mound.

Three round barrows, or possible round barrows, are present in the north-west of the parish, with two more adjacent, less than 1 kilometre distant, in Spelsbury near the Hawk Stone. There is another well-marked one, which may have been 'enhanced', near the house in Ditchley Park, and three more in a small group just outside the south-eastern tip of the parish.

The Iron Age

In southern England this period is characterized by the development of hill-forts of which Oxfordshire boasts sixteen. These enormous structures often enclosed an area of several hectares with one to three concentric rings of high ramparts and deep ditches. Our nearest, Knollbury, 7 kilometres south-west of Enstone, is a minor one of 1.5 hectares with a single rectangular rampart.

'Banjo' enclosures, frequently seen in aerial photographs, are the commonest type of Iron Age enclosure in the Cotswolds, and are so called because of their shape. There is a round area, some 100 metres in diameter and outlined by a ditch and bank, in which the large roundhouses were placed. Two other boundary lines, up to several hundred metres long, diverge from the single entrance and are thought to have been to control livestock movement. Eight banjo enclosures have already been sighted in the parish and more could yet be found. None has been excavated. There are also a further twenty-eight miscellaneous features within a 6-kilometre radius of the parish church that are enclosures or parts of trackways of uncertain age and function that need to be investigated on the ground. They could range from Bronze Age to Roman in origin.

In sharp contrast to the long barrows and round barrows of the preceding eras, there are no recognized Iron Age burial monuments in central southern Britain. The only human remains that are found often appear to have been ritually placed in disused storage pits, in ditches, or under ramparts. There are no such records yet for Enstone.

Finally, Grim's Ditch is a unique feature, 10 kilometres in diameter, that appears to enclose part of the former southern tongue of the parish in Ditchley Park and parts of adjacent parishes. It consists of segments of a Late Iron Age bank and ditch. It is uncertain whether it enclosed an urban settlement *(oppidum)* or was a loop in a defensive system between tribal areas. By the time of the Roman Conquest (AD 43) Enstone is thought to have lain in the territory of the Dobunni. The Catuvellauni to the south may have had a northerly outlier bounded by Grim's Ditch.

The Roman Period

The Roman Conquest brought tremendous changes in government, commerce, communications, and building. Although the preceding Iron Age culture appears to have been swept away, life for the common people in the countryside probably changed only gradually. Parts of the Cotswolds, including our area, were favoured for settlement by the Romans themselves and later by prosperous Romano-British families. The region was intensively farmed from large farmsteads which have become known as villas.

Enstone Parish holds the well-known villa site in Watt's Well Field 1.5 kilometres south-east of Ditchley Park, excavated in 1935. It was the first such villa farm to be studied, and also one of the first excavations carried out with the aid of aerial photography to provide a clear plan of the wall foundations before digging began. The site was already known and mentioned by the Reverend John Jordan in his account of the parish in 1857.

The excavator, Ralegh Radford, interpreted the site as a Roman settlement begun in forest in AD 70 but in touch with the commercial life of the Roman province (evidence from imported continental pottery) and probably connected to the new road (Akeman Street) 2 kilometres to the south. A rectangular enclosure, surrounded by a bank and ditch to restrain livestock, contained a wooden house and other simple buildings. About thirty years later this was rebuilt and enlarged to provide a comfortable and prosperous farm, which eventually burned down 100 years later still.

After some delay, the farmhouse was rebuilt as a two-storey stone house with colonnaded entrance and solid floors. Surprisingly, there is no sign of a bath house. Possibly water was scarce. The rest of the original enclosure was now laid out as a garden. Coin finds show that the site was occupied until about the time that the Roman legions were withdrawn from Britain in AD 410, when there are signs of economic problems. The supply of coins for everyday business was not being renewed. Those in circulation were becoming increasingly scarce, and people were hoarding them. Three hoards have been unearthed within a few hundred metres of the villa. The biggest was only 30 metres outside the later parish boundary. Farming may have continued on the site during the fifth century but the house, like others in the area, gradually decayed without being burned or sacked. Much of the land that the Romans farmed reverted to woodland or 'waste' and remained so until after the Norman Conquest more than six centuries later.

There are thought to be altogether nine Roman living sites within 6 kilometres of the parish church. These are either areas with abundant Roman potshards, or wall foundations. Other enclosures, interpreted as Roman, are visible as crop marks. There are also scattered records of coins and pottery, and a fragment of characteristic hypocaust tile from an under-floor heating system was found close to the Parish Hall. There is a possible pottery kiln site just north of Fulwell.

Farming in the Parish

Since the Parish Survey of 1971, there has been an enormous change in the structure of local farming, and in the pattern of rural employment. There are now no tenant farmers at all, whereas previously there were five who, between them, covered about half the parish. The largest of them was Jack (Taffy) Hughes who was the irascible anti-hero of Sheila Stewart's book about Mont Abbott. Taffy Hughes employed more men than are now working full-time on the land in all of the parish. Tenancies have been largely replaced by 'share-farming' arrangements locally. Share-farming is a system whereby landowners have a short-term contract with farmers for the use of their land (but not houses). The costs and profits are shared between the landowners and farmers.

Tom Walkenshaw farms all the western end of our parish, and the Elliot family share-farm the southern, Ditchley part. Between, apart from the northern part of the airfield which is farmed by Great Tew Estate, are family farms, most of which have diversified to enable them to survive. At the eastern corner of the parish, Frank Henderson, son of the famous 'Farming Ladder' Frank,[1] has built a range of factories in which Cherry Products build farm machinery and employ about twenty-five persons. Another example of diversification is David Parris's horse livery at Stone Farm. At Radford, the stone barns that once housed cart horses and grain in sheaves or sacks, now hum with computers and electronics where another twenty-five are employed. The farm here could raise a cricket team in 1920 but, in 1971, it only employed one full-time man, as it still does. At Whiteways Quarry there is now the Bennetton works, with 250 staff, emphasizing not only the increase in jobs in the parish but the change in their nature.

The cause of such change has been largely economic. The fortunes of farming have waxed and waned but the overall tendency is towards lower commodity prices, making smaller farms uneconomical. Corn

---

1 *The Farming Ladder*, a book that won national fame in the 1950s and '60s was the success story of two impecunious but determined urban boys who started from scratch at Oathill Farm before the war. It became the bible for aspiring young farmers.

growing is the main enterprise now, together with oilseed rape which would have been a rarity in the early 1970s and yields have improved markedly since then. Flax (linseed) and fodder beans and peas are also grown. Some fields are set-aside. The price of barley, which was £32 a ton in 1970/71, was in 1998 only about £64 which means that half a ton would employ and house an employee for a week then whereas more than 5 tons is today's equivalent. Beef, lambs, milk, and pigs are similar so large-scale operations are becoming inevitable despite CAP support. The results are that, unfortunately, there are fewer livestock enterprises than there once were, with no dairy herds remaining (Lady Higgs sold the last herd in 1998).

Bob Brickall operates an 'old world' farming system at Gagingwell and Cleveley – an all-grass method with sheep, Shire horses, and Aberdeen Angus and other cattle. He has had a lifelong interest in Shires and owns a private collection of horse-drawn farm equipment.

Incidentally, there are records of corn sold at Radford in the 1820s for £20 per ton which was an exceptionally high price and must have meant many hungry people. Wheat was sold from Radford in the mid-1960s for the same amount. Nowadays, wheat represents only about 13 per cent of a loaf's cost, so more than that is probably spent on its wrapping! In the Hendersons' books it was proposed that selling corn from a farm should be a criminal offence, and that it should all be fed to livestock to produce manure and increase the land's fertility. That would be difficult to achieve now!

Exceptions to purely commercial farmers are those who have developed other enterprises, or who do not depend on the land for a living. A recent example is that of Sheila Lye at Windy Hill Farm who, until lately, bred Oxford Down sheep and did so to a very high standard (She decided to use 'Heythrop' as a flock prefix, and then later found that it had been used for the same breed by the Brasseys at Heythrop many years ago.)

A different method of coping with the modern economic scene is that of Michael Jefferies at Abbey Farm, Gagingwell, who farms on a considerable scale, by contracts and share-farming, largely outside the parish. One part of his work consists of transporting and spreading chicken litter from the intensive chicken factory, Faccenda, which is a recent arrival and in marked contrast to the traditional farming of the Ivings nearby. It is perhaps surprising how unspoilt the parish is, having been spared any large-scale hedge removal, and with the landowners largely sympathetic to conservation.

Field Names

The accompanying map (see inside back cover), part of one prepared by the Enstone Local History Circle, was published in *Oxoniensa*, vols XVII/XVIII in 1952–53. Some names then omitted were published later in vol. XXI, 1956. Those omissions have been drawn into the map here which covers only the immediate surroundings of the Enstones.

The names *Victory Ground, Armistice Acres,* and *Peace Piece* refer to World War I, and were invented by Nathaniel Parsons when he bought the land in about 1920. *Cats Barn* is probably a corruption of 'Catsbrain', the name for a coarse soil of rough clay mixed with stones. *Collings Ground* could tentatively be identified with Thomas Collona, the Cleveley holder in the thirteenth century of a name that later became 'Collins'. But conjecture is risky in such cases. *Duck Puddle* might have meant what it says, or could have grown out of a corruption of Old English *Docce*, or sorrel. *Furland Field* is a corruption of Old English *furlang*, or furlong. *Hind Jones* is curious. R. T. Lattey thought that, as the name Jones is not unknown in these parts, this might be a connection with the wool trade into Wales. *Lady Acre* may have been a piece of land dedicated to the service of Our Lady. Leazow is an old name for gleaning, and *Leazow Ground Common* must have been arable. *Nor Meadow* and *Top Nor Meadow* use an Old English survival simply referring to their northerly position relating to Church Enstone. *Sanfoin* derives from French *sain*, 'health giving', and *foin* 'hay'. The plant sainfoin looks like a small sweet pea, is native on limestone, and as a dried crop is good for milk cattle. The name was borrowed from French in the seventeenth century.

Finally, it was the Enclosures, most of which took place in Oxfordshire during the height of the wool trade, that turned arable land to pasture, and hence the word that recurs among field names: *Grounds*. The result of enclosures 'was the division of the former arable areas into small number of large pasture fields, known in the north Cotswolds as *Grounds*, and over these the shepherd reigned where the villagers had once sown and tilled. There rests the site of the village [i.e. the deserted village].

These great fields can often be recognized on the modern landscape, for they are markedly different both from the long narrow fields such as came with enclosure by agreement, and from the rectilinear fields created by Parliamentary enclosure.'[1]

---

[1] *The Deserted Villages of Oxfordshire* – see 'Published Sources'.

The Natural History of Enstone

Introduction

Asked what is the most characteristic visual feature of the Cotswolds, visitor and resident alike would most probably answer that it is the lovely honey-coloured limestone of which most of the houses and dry-stone walls were traditionally built. Though some might argue that Enstone is only on the eastern fringes of the Cotswolds proper, a glance at the geological map reveals that the parish is located squarely on rocks known as the Great Oolite Series, consisting mainly of the Chipping Norton Limestone, the Sharp's Hill Beds, and the Great Oolite Limestone. Where the River Glyme and its northern tributaries cut through as they flow from north-west to south-east, however, older silts, marls, and clays are revealed such as the absorbent fuller's earth that was used to remove the grease from woollen cloth in the process known as fulling (there was at least one fulling mill in the parish). And, of course, Enstone has its share of quarries, large and small, though most are now fallen into disuse, grassed over, or used as landfill sites.

The *Oxford English Dictionary* defines oolite as 'a concretionary limestone composed of small rounded granules, like the roe of a fish, each consisting of carbonate of lime around a grain of sand as a nucleus'. The word is derived from two Greek words, translating roughly as 'egg' and 'stone' respectively, and it was this resemblance of the rock to fish eggs that persuaded the early geologists to give it the name that it continues to bear. The limestone rocks of the Great Oolite Series were deposited in warm, comparatively shallow coastal seas. It is salutary to remember, as we sit snugly in our traditional cottages, that the stone of the thick walls which protect us from the biting north-easterly winds and insulate our homes so effectively against temperatures that, on winter nights, can fall to −15 °C or below, was laid down in conditions that were not dissimilar to those that prevail around the Bahamas today. Some 160 million years ago grains of sand were rolled back and forth with the motion of the coastal currents, gradually accumulating their rings of lime as the calcium carbonate precipitated out of the warm sea water. And when the sea creatures that dwelt in these seas – brachiopods, bivalves, sea urchins, sea lilies, sponges, and so on – died and their hard parts sank to the sea bed, those that were not dashed to pieces in the swell may have been fossilized and, if you keep your eyes to the ground, it is not hard to find remains of these animals of the ancient past, especially after the fields have been newly ploughed.

And it is this limestone, with the alkaline soils derived from it, on which the flora and fauna with which we are familiar locally thrive.

Climate and Habitats

Situated in central England, almost as far from the ameliorating effects of the sea as it is possible to be in Britain, anyone who has lived in the parish for more than a few years knows that we tend to have cold, wet winters, with fog, hard frosts, and snow that may sometimes be deep enough to isolate the outlying hamlets until the farmers break through. Spring is usually later than further south or west and the summers are often hot and humid with stifling air hanging in the vales. Earlier than in damper parts of the country, the limestone quickly drains and early to mid-summer may see the green of spring burned straw brown. In the last decade, night-time winter temperatures in Cleveley, for example, have fallen to −17 °C while in summer they have soared during the early afternoon to 33 °C, a temperature difference of 50 °C or 90 °F! These considerable extremes of temperature, together with the alkaline nature of the soil have a profound influence on the habitats that have evolved here and the plants and animals that dwell in them.

It is obvious enough that the area lacks coastal or estuarine habitats. There are no large rivers or lakes. Nor are there acid upland moors nor dry heaths. Though there are some small, damp, riverside marshes, there are no large expanses of reedbeds or fens and certainly, at the other extreme, there are no mountains even if parts of the area are at elevations in excess of 180 metres (600 ft). There are none of the downs that are so typical of the chalk of Wiltshire, Berkshire, or Sussex. There is no great expanse of coniferous forest such as we might find in the Scottish Highlands. So what are we left with? Surprisingly perhaps, in the light of the above, quite a lot which is why the bird list includes more than 80 regularly seen species, for example. We do have grazing meadows and hedgerows, areas of set-a-side, coniferous and broad-leaved woods of different sizes and ages, small rivers, streams, brooks, ditches, and large ponds, wells, mill races, abandoned allotments, old airfields, a variety of gardens, arable fields around which fringes are left where no herbicides or pesticides have been used, leafy lanes and footpaths, and so on.

Birds of Enstone

This is not intended to be a complete or exhaustive list (it includes 83 of the 400 or so species on the complete British list) and it omits vagrants, accidentals, occasional visitors, and passage migrants but is intended as a guide to those species that the average birdwatcher could reasonably expect to see or hear in the parish. Where it is of interest, alternative common names have been given in parentheses and where it may not be obvious that a bird is a winter or a summer visitor, that is noted in square brackets.

Little Grebe (Dabchick) *Tachybaptus ruficollis*
Grey Heron *Ardea cinerea*
Mute Swan *Cygnus olor*
Canada Goose *Branta canadensis*
Greylag Goose *Anser anser*
Mallard *Anas platyrhyncos*
Buzzard *Buteo buteo*
Sparrowhawk *Accipiter nisus*
Kestrel *Falco tinnunculus*
Red-legged Partridge *Alectoris rufa*
Partridge *Perdix perdix*
Pheasant *Phasianus cochicus*
Moorhen *Gallinula chloropus*
Coot *Fulica atra*
Lapwing *Vanellus vanellus* [declined in recent years]
Snipe *Gallinago gallinago*
Herring Gull *Larus argentatus*
Black-headed Gull *Larus ridibundus*
Stock Dove *Columba oenas*
Wood Pigeon *Columba palumbus*
Turtle Dove *Streptopelia turtur*

Collared Dove *Streptopelia decaocto*
Cuckoo *Cuculus canorus*
Little Owl *Athene noctua*
Tawny Owl *Strix aluco*
Barn Owl *Tyto alba*

The barn owl

Swift *Apus apus* [declined in recent years]
Kingfisher *Alcedo atthis*
Green Woodpecker *Picus viridis*
Great Spotted Woodpecker *Dendrocopos major*

Lesser Spotted Woodpecker
  Dendrocopos minor
Skylark *Alauda arvensis*
Swallow *Hirundo rustica*
House Martin *Delichon urbica*
Meadow Pipit *Anthus pratensis*
Yellow Wagtail *Motacilla flava*
  [summer visitor]
Grey Wagtail *Motacilla cinerea*
Pied Wagtail *Motacilla alba*
Starling *Sturnus vulgaris*
Jay *Garrulus glandarius*
Magpie *Pica pica*
Jackdaw *Corvus Monedula*
Rook *Corvus frugilegus*
Carrion Crow *Corvus corone corone*

The robin

Robin *Erithacus rubecula*
Nightingale *Luscinia megarhynchos*
Blackbird *Turdus merula*

The blackbird

The carrion crow

Redwing *Turdus iliacus*
  [winter visitor]
Songthrush *Turdus philomelos*
Mistle Thrush *Turdus viscivorus*
Fieldfare *Turdus pilaris*
  [winter visitor]
Marsh Tit *Parus palustris*

Wren *Troglodytes troglodytes*
Dunnock (Hedge Sparrow)
  Prunella modularis
Garden Warbler *Sylvia borin*
Blackcap *Sylvia atricapilla*
Whitethroat *Sylvia communis*
Willow Warbler
  Phylloscopus trochilus
Chiffchaff *Phylloscopus collybita*
Wood Warbler *Phylloscopus sibilatrix*
Goldcrest *Regulus regulus*
Spotted Flycatcher
  Muscicapa striata
Redstart *Phoenicurus phoenicurus*

The mistle thrush

The great tit

Willow Tit *Parus montanus*
Blue Tit *Parus caeruleus*
Coal Tit *Parus ater*
Great Tit *Parus major*
Long-tailed Tit *Aegithalos caudatus*
Nuthatch *Sitta europaea*
Treecreeper *Certhia familiaris*
House Sparrow *Passer domesticus*
Tree Sparrow *Passer montanus*
Chaffinch *Fringilla fringilla*
Brambling *Fringilla montifringilla*
  [winter visitor]
Bullfinch *Pyrrhula pyrrhula*
Greenfinch *Carduelis chloris*
Siskin *Carduelis spinus*
  [winter visitor]
Goldfinch *Carduelis carduelis*
Linnet *Acanthis cannabina*
Corn Bunting *Emberiza calandra*
  [once common, now increasingly rare]
Reed Bunting *Emberiza schoeniclus*
Yellowhammer *Emberiza citrinella*

The goldfinch

Wild Flowers of Enstone

As any gardener in our parish who has attempted to grow blue hydrangeas or rhododendrons will know, success is unlikely without the addition to the soil of copious quantities of peat or other acidic compost, for ours is largely a lime-rich substrate, and the wild flora of Enstone also reflects that fact. And, as has already been outlined, the soils can be saturated in wet winters while drying almost rock hard in summer while the weather may range from severe frost to humid heat. These several factors bear on the wild flowers that are likely to grow here.

As in the case of the 'Birds of Enstone' the list below is not intended to be a complete 'Flora of the Parish of Enstone' but it aims to provide an overview of the wild flowers that the average 'stroller-about-Enstone' might reasonably expect to encounter along roadside verge, in hedgerow, in field and meadow, beside footpath or stream, or in woods and copses. Included in the list are some 125 species which is only a fraction of those on the British list but, for those who care to look more closely, many other species are to be identified in the parish. Fully aquatic species are not included.

Mistletoe *Viscum album*
Nettle *Urtica dioica*
Common Sorrel *Rumex acetosa*
Broad-leafed Dock
  Rumex obtusifolius
Greater Stitchwort *Stellaria holostea*
Common Chickweed *Stellaria media*
Bladder Campion *Silene vulgaris*
Red Campion *Silene dioica*
White Campion *Silene alba*
Ragged Robin *Lychnis flos-cuculi*
Green Hellebore *Helleborus viridis*
Marsh Marigold (May Blobs, Molly
  Blobs) *Caltha palustris*
Meadow Buttercup
  Ranunculus acris
Creeping Buttercup
  Ranunculus repens
Lesser Celandine
  Ranunculus ficaria

Traveller's Joy (Old Man's Beard)
  Clematis vitalba
Wood Anemone *Anemone nemorosa*
Common Poppy *Papaver rhoeas*
Cuckoo Flower *Cardamine pratensis*
Garlic Mustard [Jack-among-the
  Hedgerow] *Alliaria petiolata*
Perennial Honesty *Lunaria rediviva*
Shepherd's Purse
  Capsella bursa-pastoris
Wild Mignonette *Reseda lutea*
Meadowsweet *Filipendula ulmaria*
Agrimony *Agrimonia eupatoria*
Dog Rose *Rosa canina*
Bramble *Rubus fruticosus*
Wild Strawberry *Fragaria vesca*
Herb Bennet *Geum urbanum*
Silverweed *Potentilla anserina*
Crab Apple *Malus sylvestris*
Hawthorn *Crataegus monogyna*

Blackthorn *Prunus spinosa*
Tufted Vetch *Vicia cracca*
Common Vetch *Vicia sativa*
Meadow Vetchling
　Lathyrus pratensis
Sainfoin *Onobrychis viciifolia*
Ribbed Melilot *Melilotus officinalis*
Birdsfoot Trefoil *Lotus corniculatus*
Black Medick *Medicago lupulina*
Red Clover *Trifolium pratense*
White Clover *Trifolium repens*
Meadow Cranesbill
　Geranium pratense
Herb Robert *Geranium robertianum*
Hedgerow Cranesbill
　Geranium pyrenaicum
Wood Spurge
　Euphorbia amygdaloides
Dog's Mercury *Mercurialis perennis*
Himalayan Balsam
　Impatiens glandulifera
Musk Mallow *Malva moschata*
Common Mallow *Malva sylvestris*
Perforate St John's Wort
　Hypericum perforatum
Sweet Violet *Viola odorata*
Common Dog Violet
　Viola riviniana
White Bryony *Bryonia cretica*
Rosebay Willowherb
　Epilobium angustifolium
Great Willowherb
　Epilobium hirsutum
Purple Loosestrife
　Lythrum salicaria
Ivy *Hedera helix*
Cow Parsley *Anthriscus sylvestris*
Upright Hedge Parsley
　Torilis japonica
Wild Carrot *Daucus carota*
Ground Elder

Aegopodium podagraria
Hogweed *Heracleum sphondylium*
Wild Parsnip *Pastinaca sativa*
Primrose *Primula vulgaris*
Cowslip *Primula veris*
Lesser Periwinkle *Vinca minor*
Hedge Bindweed *Calystegia sepium*
Field Bindweed
　Convolvulus arvensis
Crosswort *Cruciata laevipes*
Hedge Bedstraw *Galium mollugo*
Common Comfrey
　Symphytum officinale
Field Forgetmenot *Myosotis arvensis*
Self-heal *Prunella vulgaris*
Ground Ivy *Glechoma hederacea*
White Dead-nettle *Lamium album*
Red Dead-nettle
　Lamium purpureum
Yellow Archangel
　Lamiastrum galeobdolon
Hedge Woundwort *Stachys sylvatica*
Water Mint *Mentha aquatica*
Corn Mint *Mentha arvensis*
Common Calamint
　Calamintha sylvatica
Bittersweet [Woody Nightshade]
　Solanum dulcamera
Dark Mullein *Verbascum nigrum*
Common Toadflax *Linaria vulgaris*
Ivy-leaved Toadflax
　Cymbalaria muralis
Foxglove *Digitalis purpurea*
Germander Speedwell
　Veronica chamaedrys
Common Field Speedwell
　Veronica persica
Greater Plantain *Plantago major*
Ribwort Plantain
　Plantago lanceolata
Red Valerian *Centranthus ruber*

Dwarf Elder *Sambucus ebulus*
Wayfaring Tree *Viburnum lantana*
Honeysuckle *Lonicera periclymenum*
Field Scabious *Knautia arvensis*
Teasel *Dipsacus fullonum*
Nettle-leaved Bellflower
  Campanula trachelium
Canadian Golden-rod
  Solidago virgurea
Daisy *Bellis perennis*
Scentless Mayweed
  Tripleurospermum inodorum
Michaelmas Daisy *Aster novi-belgii*
Butterbur *Petasites hybridus*
Yarrow *Achillea millefolium*
Ox-eye Daisy *Leucanthemum vulgare*
Ragwort *Senecio jacobaea*
Groundsel *Senecio vulgaris*
Burdock *Arctium minus/lappa*
Spear Thistle *Cirsium vulgare*
Meadow Thistle *Cirsium dissectum*
Musk Thistle *Carduus nutans*

Welted Thistle *Carduus acanthoides*
Greater Knapweed
  Centaurea scabiosa
Chicory *Cichorium intybus*
Perennial Sowthistle
  Sonchus arvensis
Dandelion *Taraxacum spp.*
Rough Hawkbit *Leontodon hispidus*
hawkweeds *Hieracium spp.*
hawksbeards *Crepis spp.*
Ramsons *Allium ursinum*
Bluebell *Endymion non-scriptus*
Black Bryony *Tamus communis*
Common Solomon's Seal
  Polygonatum multiflorum
Snowdrop *Galanthus nivalis*
Lords and Ladies

[The compiler of this list has not observed any orchid species in the area.]

Other Wildlife

While some people are fascinated by fungi (not only for culinary purposes), such as the Field Mushroom, Shaggy Inkcap, or Puffballs that are to be found in the area, and others may be in awe of the age and stature of trees (for those who like to make wine from the flowers and berries of Elders, for example, or cordial or fritters from the flowers, there is no shortage!), for most wanderers on the wild side it is flowers and birds that command attention. Nonetheless, it is worth looking at some of the other highlights of Enstone's wildlife.

Invertebrates, including insects, are of interest mainly to gardeners – unless they bite or sting – but, though they rarely arrive in such numbers as they once did in spring and summer, butterflies still brighten our warm-weather days and, as summers seem to grow still warmer and more humid, species, such as the brightly coloured Clouded Yellow *(Colias croceus)* may turn up as early as May though most migrants from Europe arrive in August on intermittent years. Among the first butterflies to be seen, however, are the Small White *(Artogeia rapae)* and the pretty Orange-tip *(Anthocharis cardamines)*, while the lemon-yellow Brimstone *(Gonepteryx rhamni)* may be seen in two waves, April to May after hibernation and then the new generation in July to September. Perhaps one of the gardener's pet hates of the butterfly world is the Large White *(Pieris brassicae)*, that may be seen from May to October, for its black-spotted yellow caterpillars can quickly ruin a whole cabbage patch and will eat most brassicas. One of our most spectacular – and quite common – butterflies is the Peacock *(Inachis io)* with its four noticeable eye spots. At rest, however, it is easy to overlook for the undersides of its wings closely resemble dead leaves. Once again it appears in two waves: March–June and July–October. Painted Ladies *(Vanessa cardui)* and Small Tortoiseshells *(Aglais urticae)* could be confused at a cursory glance but look out for the latter especially on Buddliea. In some years, Painted Ladies may be rare in this area or even absent altogether. Another spectacular member of the Nymphalid family to be found here and throughout the British Isles is the Red Admiral *(Vanessa atalanta)* with its velvety black upper wings decorated with four broad, reddish-orange bands and white blotches. Again, adults are fond of feeding on Buddlieas. Two of our more common butterflies are the Gatekeeper *(Pyronia tithonus)* – thought to get its name from its habit of settling on gateposts – and the similar but larger and more dull-coloured Meadow Brown *(Maniola jurtina)*. In our woods, woodland edges, and other shady places, the cream-dappled, brown butterfly with white-centred black spot near each wing tip, the Speckled Wood *(Pararge aegeria)* is surprisingly common throughout the spring and summer, and it also seems to find its way into gardens or even our houses. And in these areas, too, you may see the occasional Ringlet *(Aphantopus hyperantus)* or ragged-winged Comma *(Polygonia c-album)* named for the whitish comma-shaped mark on the underside of each wing. An unmistakable species that is on the wing in the parish between June/July and August is the Marbled White *(Melanargia galathea)*, Britain's only black-and-white butterfly – look for them especially on the flowers of Knapweed. On grassy tracks and woodland rides, you should see the Common Blue Butterfly *(Polyommatus icaurus)* but remember that, as in the case of many so-called 'blues', the females are brown. It is also likely that you will spot a skipper or two and the occasional fritillary.

There are many species of moths to be seen in the parish and not all of them are nocturnal. One of the most conspicuous – though it seems to have declined in recent years – is the Six-spot Burnet *(Zygaena filipendula)* which is attracted to knapweeds, thistles, and scabious, its bright colours advertising the fact that it is very poisonous to eat.

Another feature of the area in and around meadows and arable fields in April and May (especially 25 April!) are the dense swarms of dangling-legged Common St Mark's Flies (25 April is St Mark's Day). Dragonflies and damselflies are often spectacular and highly coloured, and may be seen some distance from water, especially the large Southern Hawker *(Aeshna cyanea)* which is on the wing from June to October or even into November in milder years.

And if you are sitting in the garden on a warm evening any time between May and July, do not be disturbed by the low, buzzing drone of an insect that seems to be too big to fly – it is only a harmless Cockchafer or Maybug *(Melolontha melolontha)*. Though the larvae can be a serious pest of crops and garden plants, these days, they seldom occur in sufficient numbers to be a problem.

Most people will be aware that, as in so many parts of Britain, locally produced honey is now at a premium. This is because many populations of Honey Bees *(Apis mellifera)*, including 'wild' colonies, have been decimated by a parasitic mite that invades the hives.

And, among other invertebrates, the plethora of slugs and snails (some of the latter with delightfully coloured shells) are the bane of every Enstone gardener's life.

Turning to other vertebrates, anyone living in Cleveley will be aware of the presence of Common Frogs *(Rana temporaria)* and Common Toads *(Bufo bufo)*, especially in early spring when the adults are on their mating migrations from their winter quarters to rivers and ponds. Sadly, it is not uncommon to see them squashed on the roads, even though the volume of traffic in the area is light. Frogs and toads are easily distinguished: a frog has a soft, smooth, damp skin and long hind legs on which it travels by leaping; a toad has a dry, warty skin, shorter legs, and tends to walk rather than 'leapfrog'.

Britain has only three species of snake: the harmless Grass Snake *(Natrix natrix)* which is certainly to be found in the parish: the venomous Adder *(Vipera berus)* which one would expect to find in drier, rockier, warmer locations and which helps to keep down populations of verminous rodents; and the rare Smooth Snake *(Coronella austriaca)*, a heathland animal not found here. Doubtless, too, there are the legless lizards, the snake-like Slow-worms *(Anguis fragilis)* which were once so common even in gardens. And one would expect Common Lizards to be present.

Britain has roughly seventy species of mammals – compared with more than 4000 worldwide, so our islands are not well represented. Of the world's mammals about one-quarter are bats and, in this respect, Britain reflects the world average though a number of species are now rare but, because bats are small, secretive, and night-flying, it is not always easy to realize their importance. Anyone walking around the lanes and byways of our parish on a warm summer's evening, however, should see them in some numbers as they flit past searching for their insect prey. Of course, British bats are quite harmless, all species are protected, and they don't get caught in the hair – their sonar is far to sensitive for that!

Once again, as road deaths will confirm, we do have a reasonable population of Hedgehogs *(Erinaceous europaeus)* and the hills and ridges of disturbed earth in lawns, banks, and meadows are evidence of the frequency of Moles *(Talpa europaea)*. With their long snouts, the insectivorous shrews *(Sorex spp.)* are easy to identify with the Pygmy species *(S. minutus)* measuring only up to 60 mm (2.3 in) excluding its tail.

Rabbits *(Oryctolagus cuniculus)* abound everywhere, though there has been mention of a new disease that is reducing their populations countrywide, and the Brown Hare *(Lepus capensis)* is surprisingly common in and around the parish – especially noticeable in spring. Red Squirrels *(Sciurus vulgaris)* do not occur and, although its New World cousin, the Grey Squirrel *(S. carolinensis),* is quite common, its presence in some parts of the parish does not seem to be as visible as it is in other areas of England. Sadly, as well as House Mice, resident cats will also bring in Bank Voles *(Clethrionomys glareolus)* and Field Voles *(Microtus agrestis)* – voles may be distinguished by their blunt noses, chunky rather round-shouldered bodies, short tails and ears. And, as in so many parts of the country now, Water Voles *(Arvicola terrestris)* do not seem to grace our waterways – where would Kenneth Grahame (1859–1932) have found his original for 'Ratty' in *Wind in the Willows* today?

Common or Brown Rats *(Rattus norvegicus)* are quite common and, in places such as the lake at Cleveley, pose a threat to the young of waterbirds. Wood Mice and the Yellow-necked Mouse are difficult to find at the best of times and the compiler of this survey is unaware of any Harvest Mice in the area.

The Red Fox *(Vulpes vulpes)* is quite common though, in the countryside today, they are often less visible than they are in urban areas where they feed from dustbins and the like and may often be seen gallivanting in suburban streets and gardens at night. Weasels *(Mustela nivalis)* and Stoats *(M. erminea)* are to be found here though the smaller Weasel seems to be more apparent. And there have been occasional sightings of the much larger Polecat *(M. putorius)*. Britain's largest mustelid, the Badger *(Meles meles)* is certainly quite common in the area as, once again, their carcasses on the main roads are evidence. But, if you look carefully among banks and hedgerows, you will see evidence of their activity including occupied sets, diggings, and recently used dung pits. And any wanderers late at night or early in the morning may even sight individuals trotting along our lanes.

There are Fallow Deer *(Cervus dama)* in the Ditchley area but the compiler is not certain if they venture into the parish with the Roe Deer *(Capreolus capreolus)* which are present in the woodlands here. More likely to be seen are the small, but surprisingly bold, Muntjac *(Muntiacus reevesi)* with their small antlers and, in the males, slender 'tusks' in the upper jaw. Muntjacs are easy to identify, being hardly larger than a fox and with a characteristically rounded back. Despite their small size, they make a very loud barking call. This species was introduced into parks and gardens from eastern China.

Other Reading

The standard work on Enstone is the Reverend John Jordan's *Parochial History,* published in 1857 and now rarely to be found. It provided a footing for this present book and is a rich mine for parish records, the originals now being held in the County Archives at Oxford.

Once, and perhaps once only in its long history, Enstone achieved general notoriety. This was on the occasion of the visit of King Charles I and Henrietta Maria to 'the Goldwell, which Bushell formed his waterworks at'. There are references to Mr Bushell, the occasion, and to what became known as Queen Henrietta's Waterworks in the writings of John Aubrey, John Evelyn, Antony à Wood, and Robert Plot. Later on, Robert Graves used all of these as sources for a masterly reconstruction of the royal visit in his *Wife to Mr Milton* (1943).

Sheila Stewart's *Lifting the Latch* (1987) is a 'story of life on the land' carefully crafted from recorded conversations with an Enstone shepherd, Mont Abbott, whose recollections of life in the parish between the world wars are the living stuff of history, and are much quoted here.

There are entries for Enstone, Cleveley, Radford, and Lidstone in John Kibble's *Wychwood Forest* and its *Border Places,* another work of character, first published in 1928 and republished by The Wychwood Press in 1999. Mention must also be made of the *Enstone Village Appraisal* (1995) which recorded the changes that took place in the parish during the second half of the twentieth century. This is the source for contemporary references and data at the time of writing. Lastly, no work of this nature can be attempted without reference to Jennifer Sherwood and Nikolaus Pevsner's *Oxfordshire*.

Other source material, much of it previously unpublished, has come from the archive of the Enstone Local History Circle.

GB

Published Sources

Allison, K. J., et al., *The Deserted Villages of Oxfordshire* (Leicester University Press, 1965).

Bond, C. J., *The Rural Settlements of Mediaeval England*, ed. Aston, Austin, and Dyer (Blackwell, 1989).

Briggs, G., Cook, J., and Rowley, T., *The Archaeology of the Oxford Region* (Open University Dept of External Studies, 1986).

Corbett, Elsie, *A History of Spelsbury* (Cheney & Sons, 1962).

Ekwall, Eilert, *The Concise Oxford Dictionary of English Place Names* (Oxford University Press, 1960).

Enstone Parish Council, *Enstone – A Review* (1971).

Enstone Village Appraisal, *The Report* (1995).

Foreman, Wilfred, *Oxfordshire Mills* (Phillimore, 1983).

Gelling, Margaret, *The Place Names of Oxfordshire* (Cambridge University Press, 1953).

Graves, Robert, *Wife to Mr Milton* (Cassell, 1949).

Hammond, Nigel, *The Oxfordshire Village Book* (Countryside Books, 1983).

Jordan, The Reverend John, *A Parochial History of Enstone* (Henry Alden, 1857).

Kibble, John, *Wychwood Forest and its Border Places* (The Wychwood Press, 1999).

Morris, John (ed.), Domesday Book (of 1086) *Oxfordshire* (Phillimore, 1978).

Radford, C. A. Ralegh, 'The Roman Villa at Ditchley, Oxon', in *Oxoniensia* I (1936).

Sherwood, Jennifer and Pevsner, Nikolaus, *The Buildings of England – Oxfordshire* (1974).

Southey, Robert, *Letters from England* (Cresset Press, 1951).

Stewart, Sheila, *Lifting the Latch – The Life of Mont Abbott* (Oxford University Press, 1987).

Webb, Mary, et al., *Glyme Valley* (The Artisan Press, 1997).

Wood-Jones, Raymond B., *Traditional Domestic Architecture in the Banbury Region* (Manchester University Press, 1963).

Enstone in 1854

From the Post Office Directory of Berkshire & Oxfordshire, 1854

ENSTONE consisting of the Hamlets of CHURCH ENSTONE, NEAT ENSTONE, LIDSTONE, CHALFORD, CLEVELEY, GAGINGWELL, and RADFORD.

ENSTONE is an extensive parish, consisting of the hamlets or townships of CHURCH ENSTONE, NEAT ENSTONE, LIDSTONE, CHALFORD, CLEVELEY, GAGINGWELL, and RADFORD, it is 15 miles north-west of Oxford, 5 south-east from Chipping Norton, and 72½ from London, in the Hundred of Chadlington, on the river Glyme, and in the Union of Chipping Norton. The living is a rectory and vicarage, in the deanery of Chipping Norton, archdeaconry of Oxford, and in the diocese of Oxford. The rectory formerly belonged to Winchcombe Abbey, in Gloucestershire, but now belongs to the College of Christ Church, Oxford, is impropriate, and possesses the great tithes, commuted for an annual rent-charge of £1,244, besides a good glebe of 53 acres. The vicarage possesses a rent charge of £300, an endowment from the rectory of £16, a glebe of 25 acres, and a good house. The patron of the vicarage is Viscount Dillon, and the incumbent is the Rev. John Jordan. The population of the parish, in 1851, was 1249; acreage 6,185, the principal part being arable. The lord of the manor is Viscount Dillon. There is a valuable estate belonging to the parish for charitable uses, the first being the repairs of the church, the title deeds connected with which are very ancient, some being 500 years old, and amongst them is one granting freedom to a man, one John Hobbes, who is thereby manumitted "ab omni juge servitudinis et ab omni vinculo villano."

CHURCH ENSTONE contains the parish church, which is a very ancient structure, dedicated to St. Kenelm, and has a handsome Norman doorway, some very good transition Norman piers and arches in the interior, several other remarkable antiquities, as an original altar and reredos, part of the rood loft &c., and a good tower and peal of bells. There are also National schools for boys and girls. The population, in 1851, was 263.

NEAT ENSTONE, sometimes called ROAD ENSTONE, from the circumstances of the high road to Birmingham and Worcester passing through it, has its name Neat from the herds of neat cattle that in ancient times were depastured on its open fields and commons. It is half a mile south of Church Enstone, 5 miles south-west of Chipping Norton, and 72 from London. Here were some famous waterworks, recently destroyed, that were constructed by Thomas Bushel, servant to Lord Bacon, and which were visited with much pomp by Charles I. and his Queen, while resident in the neighbourhood in 1636. There is a small Methodist chapel here; a Baptist chapel at Cleveley, and a Roman Catholic chapel at Radford.

Church Enstone

GENTRY
    Jordan, Rev. John, Vicarage
    Oakley Mrs. Esther
    Price Robert, esq

TRADERS
    Adkins John, shopkeeper
    Arthur John, *'Marshall's Arms'*
    Bennett Edward, shoemaker
    Bennett Thomas, tailor
    Brown James, shoemaker
    Checkley Jonas, farmer
    Dowdeswell Isaac, saddler
    Draper William & Thomas, blacksmiths
    Drinkwater Richard, farmer
    Gregory John, baker
    Hartley John, miller & farmer
    Hawtin Thomas, carpenter
    Jones William, shoemaker
    Steel Joseph, farmer
    Taylor Stephen, *'Crown'* & carrier
    Letters through Neat Enstone

Neat Enstone

TRADERS
    Aldridge Charles, painter & glazier
    Austin Thomas, grocer
    Baker Thomas, *'Bell'* & plasterer
    Bennett Edward, sen. shoemaker
    Bennett John, shopkeeper
    Bennett Thomas William, carpenter
    Blackwell John, farrier
    Blackwell Joseph, farmer
    Brown John, farmer
    Cattell Edward, *Lichfield Arms commercial inn & posting house, & farmer*
    Cleaver John, shoemaker
    Collins William, shopkeeper & carrier
    Collins William, mason
    Dossett William Talbot commercial inn & posting house
    Gardner Thomas, tailor

Griffin Edward, *'Harrow'*
Hall Thomas, blacksmith
Hunt William, carpenter
Jefferis William, saddler
Jolly John, farmer
Jones Robert, baker
Kibble William, grocer
& postmaster
Knight William, *'Swan'*
& butcher
Magee John, plumber, glazier
& paintr
Messer Sarah (Mrs.), plumber,
glazier & painter
Wells William, butcher &
beer retailer
Wheeler James,
gravestone cutter

Lidstone

TRADERS
Claridge Richard, farmer
Goodrich William, miller
& farmer
Lidstone mill
Harrison James, farmer
Letters through Neat Enstone

Chalford

TRADERS
Baylis Mark, farmer &
artificial manure
manufacturer, Chalford
bone mill
Baylis William, farmer
Hodges Richard, farmer
Holton Nicholas, farmer,
Broadstonehill
Letters through Neat Enstone

Cleveley

TRADERS
Baughan Daniel, wheelwright
& beer retailer
Claridge Jonathan, miller
Claridge Richard, miller
Eltham Francis, farrier
Smith Jonas, carpenter
Taylor James, farmer
Letters through Neat Enstone

Gagingwell

TRADERS
Carter Hannah (Mrs.),
'White Hart,'
Cuckolds holt
Carter Thomas, farmer
Sanders William, farmer
Wilsdon Albert, farmer
Letters through Neat Enstone

Radford

Bowden Miss Mary
Winter Rev. Edward Warden
[catholic]
Lester Susanna (Mrs.), miller
& farmer
Parsons Nathaniel, farmer
Letters through Neat Enstone